God's Call To Holiness

A Seven Part Presentation On Holiness From The Wesleyan Perspective

By

Richard M. Bradley

GOD'S CALL TO HOLINESS
ISBN: 978-1-60416-988-1

First Printing November 2012

Reformation Publishers
242 University Drive
Prestonsburg, Kentucky 41653
1-800-765-2464
rpublisher@aol.com

Printed in the United States of America

Preface

1 Thessalonians 4:7
For God hath not called us unto uncleanness,
but unto holiness.
KJV

What God **DEMANDS** cannot be **OPTIONAL** with us! Therefore...when God says, **"Be ye holy......."** there is placed before the child of God a **SPIRITUAL IMPERATIVE** from which there can be no escape!

1 Pet 1:16
Because it is written, Be ye holy; for I am holy. (KJV)

God intended from the beginning that **HOLINESS of heart** should be the **"NORM"** of Christian experience and conduct. Nothing less can satisfy the requirements of Christian discipleship! Yet today in the Reformation Movement of the Church of God, we are finding that **HOLINESS** is a word that has fallen on hard times. The attitude pervades and prevails that HOLINESS/SANCTIFICATION is **OPTIONAL!**

It is in this vein of thinking that I began to put together this series of lessons on *"God's Call To Holiness"* for a minister's retreat and for lessons to be taught in day time conferences in a couple of camp meetings which I served as evangelist. At the urging of many I have now sought to get this material into the hands of pastors and any child of God. My endeavor is to place within their reach something which may be a help to them in their service to our great God.

It is given in the spirit in which it was received, freely. Use it as you wish and if you find no merit in it, freely discard it. My only motive is and continues to be striving to be a blessing to the body of

Christ, the church.

Richard M. Bradley
Full-Time Church of God
Evangelist — TTE Association, Inc.
P.O. Box 65
Oak Hill, WV 25901-0065
skypilotwo@msn.com
Phone: 304 469-9247
Home 304 573-0135 Cell

Table of Contents

Lesson One

God's Call To Holiness

Leviticus 11:

44 For I am the Lord your God: ye shall therefore sanctify yourselves, and **<u>ye shall be holy; for I am holy</u>***: neither shall ye defile yourselves with any manner of creeping thing that creepeth upon the earth.*

45 For I am the Lord that bringeth you up out of the land of Egypt, to be your God: **<u>ye shall therefore be holy, for I am holy</u>***.   KJV*

1 Peter 1:16

Because it is written, **<u>Be ye holy; for I am holy.</u>** *KJV*

Hebrews 12:14

Follow peace with all men, **<u>and holiness</u>***, without which no man shall see the Lord: KJV*

1 Thessalonians 4:7

For God hath not called us unto uncleanness, **<u>but unto holiness</u>***.   KJV*

The word **"holiness"** describes the essential nature of God. One of the great Christian hymns addresses the deity of God as:

"Holy, holy, holy!   Lord God Almighty!"

And one of its lines is,

"Only Thou are holy...there is none beside Thee."

To say that God is holy is simply to say that **GOD** is **<u>GOD!</u>** Holiness means ***"separation."***

Isa 46:9

Remember the former things of old: for I am God, and there is none else; I am God, **and there is none like me,** *(KJV)*

To be holy means basically to be "***set apart*** "— it means to be "***different*** ". God is different from all things created in terms of His transcendence, His majesty, His moral perfection, and His sovereign love.

That God is holy means He is different from everything that is not God! **God alone is holy.** His holiness is unique to Him and belongs to no other, **except as He imparts it!** Thus, when any of God's creation, including human beings, are said to be holy it means they are set apart for God's exclusive use. *(This includes pastors, and parishioners.)*

Insofar as holiness may be ascribed to beings other than God, it is a derivative of God's Holiness and has its origin in Him. This means that holiness is first and foremost a religious concept and not a moral or ethical one. In other words, its primary focus is ***vertical*** rather than horizontal.

But holiness as it is progressively revealed in the Bible and pursued in the lives of human beings takes on a secondary and consequential meaning which is a moral and ethical one, **i.e.,** ***horizontal,*** affecting all our relations with other persons and with the created order.

What God **DEMANDS** cannot be **OPTIONAL** with us! Therefore.....when God says, **"Be ye holy......."** there is placed before the child of God a **SPIRITUAL IMPERATIVE** from which there can be no escape!

1 Pet 1:16

Because it is written, Be ye holy; for I am holy. (KJV)

Today in the Reformation Movement of the Church of God, we

are finding that **HOLINESS** is a word that has fallen on hard times. As I stated on the Preface page the attitude pervades and prevails that HOLINESS/SANCTIFICATION is **OPTIONAL!**

To many the doctrine of the *"in filling of the Holy Spirit"* or *"heart purity"* or *"sanctification"* is considered to be a **spiritual luxury** rather than a **spiritual necessity !** Those who have this attitude do not necessarily OPPOSE the doctrine of *"heart purity"* or *"second blessing holiness"*, but when the call goes out for seekers and possessors of this clear-cut biblical experience...... **THEY SIMPLY DO NOT RALLY TO THE CALL!**

Heb 12:14
Follow peace with all men, and holiness, without which no man shall see the Lord: (KJV)

As one holiness advocate I am very much concerned that as a movement we are losing our identity as a **"holiness people"**, and are drifting from the moorings which our pioneer brothers and sisters placed for safe keeping in our care, with the added responsibility that we pass that same torch of truth to the next generation. **It is an utter impossibility to pass on to the next generation what you do not possess in the present generation !**

God is holy with an ***absolute holiness*** that is without limitation or degree. This holiness God **cannot** impart to His creatures, but there is a relative and contingent holiness which He shares with angels in heaven and with **REDEEMED** men on earth in their preparation for living in heaven. The Bible admonishes us to be PERFECT, but that perfection is a relative perfection. In the realm of perfection there are different levels of perfection:

- **ABSOLUTE PERFECTION**, this is the highest state of perfection. None occupy this realm save God the One and ONLY HOLY ONE of the Ages.

B **ANGELIC PERFECTION**, this is the perfection of angels yet it is far below the perfection of God.

B **ADAMIC PERFECTION**, this is the perfection that Adam and Eve had *prior* to the fall. While it is totally and fully perfection it is a perfection that is a little lower than the angels.

Heb 2:7

Thou madest him a little lower than the angels; thou crownedst him

with glory and honour, and didst set him over the works of thy hands: (KJV)

B **CHRISTIAN PERFECTION**, This is a level of perfection that is lower than that of Adam and Eve before the fall, but nonetheless it is holiness perfected and higher than the world view of holiness and purity. Christian perfection is the only perfection we are supposed to have in this life. It is not expected to make us exempt for errors or humanity. Perfect love is not expected to produce a perfect body or a perfect mind. *INFALLIBILITY* is not a fruit of holiness! Holiness is only love made perfect and not judgment made infallible. We will never attain to FLAWLESSNESS C but we must be *FAULTLESS* to stand before Him

Jude 24

Now unto him that is able to keep you from falling, and to present you faultless *before the presence of his glory with exceeding joy, (KJV)*

This holiness God can and does impart to His children. He shares it with them by imputation and by impartation.

Because He has made it available to them through **the blood of His LAMB** — He requires it of men.

— ***imputation*** — the act of imputing, an attribution].
— ***impartation*** — to give; bestow: to impart, to grant a part or share of, give.

To Israel *(His Old Testament people)* first and later to His Church *(His New Testament people)* God spoke saying;

"Be ye holy; for I am holy."

He did not say "*Be ye* **AS HOLY** *as I am.*" That would be to demand of us ***absolute holiness***, something that belongs to God **ALONE**. *But He did say to us; "**Be YE** holy, **FOR** I am holy."* What are we as His disciples, His servants to do? We must like Moses of old cover ourselves with faith and humility while we strive a quick look at **WHO and WHAT God is !** We must hide our unholiness in the wounds of Christ on the Cross **[cleft of the ROCK]** even as Moses hid himself in the cleft of the rock while the glory of God passed by.

We must take refuge from God IN God!

What is the basis and essential truth about **"Holiness"** ? It is that **"holiness"** is the very character of God, and He wants His children to share in His character ! By faith and obedience, by constant meditation on the holiness of God, by hating iniquity and living righteously, by a growing acquaintance with the Spirit of Holiness, we can acclimate ourselves to the fellowship of the saints on earth and prepare ourselves for the eternal companionship of a holy God and the saints above.

I am convinced that the subject of holiness is without sequel in ranking of importance with God, and His Son, Jesus Christ on heaven's agenda.

The *Church of God Reformation Movement* came into being as a body of holiness believers. It was October 5th, 1881 in Beaver Dam, Indiana that Daniel Sidney Warner took his walk from denominationalism and sectism and took his stand in **HOLINESS** and ***Holy Spirit leadership*** for the church. How far has this reformation drifted from that holiness beginning?

At this present moment we need desperately to rediscover and to uncover the landmarks of **Holiness** for our people and help them find their bearings and gain a new/renewed vision of the world **BEHIND** us and the Kingdom **WITHIN** us and Heaven **BEFORE** us.

I do not pretend to think that I could cover all that the Bible says about Holiness in this single lesson, nor in those which are to follow, for references to the subject are inexhaustible. Just to list them would challenge the patience of a staff of catalogers. Just the word **"holy"** appears over 578 times in the Scriptures. The subject of being holy and holiness is so vital and so fills the book I have before me, that it has become known across the centuries as:

"The Book on Holiness.....The Holy Bible!"

Let us approach our subject of **"HOLINESS**....!" from these three aspects:

— **Its IMPORTANCE......**
— **Its IMPLICATIONS......**
— **Its INSISTENCE......**

I. The *IMPORTANCE* of Holiness!

There was an instance in the history of France, when the Crown Prince of France approached a village where he was met by a committee of the principle leaders of that village. They expressed to the Prince their allegiance and their great desire to have greeted his coming with appropriate fanfare, in particular, an artillery barrage. **(Similar to a 21 gun salute.)** However they informed the Prince that they had 13 reasons why they could not do so.....**the first being because their village did not own a cannon** . As they continued to enumerate reasons the Prince motioned for silence. Then he said:

"Enough my loyal friends, the single fact that you have no cannon is sufficient reason for not greeting me with a barrage of artillery. No other reason is necessary."

It is precisely so with the instruction of our text:

1 Pet 1:15-16
15 But as he which hath called you is holy, so be ye holy in all manner of conversation;
16 Because it is written, Be ye holy; for I am holy. (KJV)

Heb 12:14
Follow peace with all men, and holiness, without which no man shall see the Lord: (KJV)

If no man can see the Lord **WITHOUT HOLINESS**., then the importance of holiness is established **WITHOUT THE NEED TO RECITE ANY OTHER REASON!** Our scripture says that UNLESS A PERSON IS HOLY....He cannot see God, much less enjoy God.

"......blessed are the PURE IN HEART, for they shall see God." Matt 5:8

Ps 24:
3 Who shall ascend into the hill of the LORD? or who shall stand in his holy place?
4 They that have clean hands and pure hearts.(KJV)

Without **"HOLINESS"** no man can see God, but ***WITH***

HOLINESS any man can see Him...! Sin in anyone's heart makes the presence of a **HOLY GOD** a torment! A sinner would be of all men most miserable in the presence of a Holy God and all of the holy angels -- just as the child of God would be most miserable in the presence of the vileness of sin.

Heaven is not only a place.....***it is a SPIRIT!*** If you do not possess the spirit of Heaven in the heart then you could never enjoy the place! That is why the ***NEW BIRTH is necessary!*** **(Illus: Tobacco worm evolves into a nocturnal moth/butterfly. The worm likes the tobacco patch – the butterfly the flower garden.)**

The nature dictates when the worm/butterfly wants to be!

We ***MUST HAVE HOLINESS IN THE HEART*** then wherever we are there will be just a little bit of heaven present. Whatever it is to be holy....that is what we must be if we are to come into the presence of the *Thrice Holy God* of Eternity and enjoy His fellowship either **HERE** or **HEREAFTER !**

II. THE *IMPLICATIONS* OF HOLINESS.....!

What is IMPLIED in this **HOLINESS** that is so indispensable? What are the IMPLICATIONS of being HOLY in heart?

1. To Be HOLY Means To Be FREE FROM SIN...!

Sin exists in TWO FORMS: ***Sin as Guilt***....the result of transgressions or acts of sin committed. ***Sin as Defilement or Pollution*** .... The result of a FALLEN STATE or NATURE! HOLINESS means to be FREE from both ***the GUILT*** and ***the DEFILEMENT*** of sin.

The **BIRTH OF THE SPIRIT** does one thing in the heart of the recipient.

John 3:5

Jesus answered, Verily, verily, I say unto thee, Except a

man be born of water and of the Spirit, he cannot enter into the kingdom of God. (KJV)

The **<u>BAPTISM OF THE SPIRIT</u>** does something entirely different.

Matt 3:11

I indeed baptize you with water unto repentance: but he that cometh after me is mightier than I, whose shoes I am not worthy to bear: he shall baptize you with the Holy Ghost, and with fire: (KJV)

They are both works of the Holy Spirit but they are wrought at subsequent times in the life of the believer because of their inability to grasp all the workings of the Spirit at once.

— ***The Birth of the Spirit*** gives you something that you never had before.....ETERNAL LIFE!

— ***The Baptism of the Spirit*** will take away something that you have always had.....the ***NATURE OF THE FIRST ADAM.***

The birth MUST precede the baptism! If a birth has not taken place there is nothing to be baptized! *(This is simple logic.)*

— ***The Birth of the Spirit*** gives you PEACE WITH GOD!

— ***The Baptism of the Spirit*** gives you the PEACE OF GOD!

Rom 5:1-2

1 Therefore being justified by faith, ***<u>we have peace with God</u>*** *through our Lord Jesus Christ:*

2 By whom also we have access by faith ***<u>into this grace wherein we stand</u>****, and rejoice in hope of the glory of God. (KJV)*

— ***The Birth of the Spirit*** starts a civil war in your heart.

— ***The Baptism of the Spirit*** puts an end to that war when you give the battle over to the Lord.

2 Chr 20:15

.......Thus saith the LORD unto you, Be not afraid nor dismayed by reason of this great multitude; for the battle is not yours, but God's. (KJV)

— ***The Birth of the Spirit*** gives you power to BEGIN.
— ***The Baptism of the Spirit*** TO BE.....still, sweet, strong, patient, holy!

— ***The Birth of the Spirit*** takes you *OUT OF THE WORLD!*

— ***The Baptism of the Spirit*** takes the world OUT OF YOU! *(Moses and Children of Israel/40 years)*

[Two witnesses, testaments, crossings, compartments, veils, altars, highways, pillars, rests, lands, pitchings, Adams, arks, lives--steps down/up.]

We will never be free from the **PRESENCE OF SIN** until we get into the eternal world, but to be *HOLY* means that we can be **FREE FROM SIN** in a sinful world. In substance, this is to say that holiness means that we are to have the world taken out of us while we yet live in the world.

John 17:15

I pray not that thou shouldest take them out of the world, but that thou shouldest keep them from the evil. (KJV)

Illus: It is like a ship in the ocean. The ship can float no matter how much ocean it is in....so long as the ocean does not get in the ship. I learned that Salt Mackerel are not salty while living, The salt is added after they die to preserve them.

If God can keep a fish from becoming salty in a salty sea, He can certainly keep me from sin in a sinful world.

I have been accused of being too extreme because I preach ***that you can be saved from ALL SIN and live above sin in this life***. I plead guilty to the charge, **I am an extremist for the Lord and HOLINESS.** If you disagree with my extremism for the Lord and HOLINESS then you automatically become the opposite.....**which is an extremist for SIN!**

Your argument must become SIN ***is more powerful than God***....Satan's power to cause us to sin is greater than God's power to deliver us from and keep us from sin!

Personally, I ELECT TO BE AND EXTREMIST FOR CHRIST! How about you?

2. To Be HOLY Implies SOUL NORMALCY.....!

Sin is the invader, the thorn, the intruder in the life of man. Sin is the ***ABNORMALITY!***

(Every prison, hospital, lock, police car, asylum, broken home, addict, brothel)

HOLINESS is soul health ! It is to the spiritual man what physical health is to the physical man. It is the state in which man was made originally and the state in which he is designed to live forever!

1 Thes 4:3
For this is the will of God, even your sanctification, that ye should abstain from fornication: (KJV)

If there is a struggle in reaching the state of holiness in our lives it is the struggle of reluctance to let go and yield to the will of God.

The person themselves must possess the inner proof positive

within themselves that all is well with them physically. They know themselves better than any doctor can know them. *(STGA (acronym) Something That's Going Around —Try this for a week)* I have said that to say this: **HOLINESS IS SOUL HEALTH!**

— It is the state in which the believer is enabled to live the Christian life WITHOUT pain, discomfort and struggle.

— It is the state in which one can truly say, "I delight in the will of God!

His yoke IS EASY, His burden IS LIGHT, His commandments ARE NOT GRIEVOUS!"

— It is the place in the Christian life where one does what he likes....and still does right...for THE DESIRE TO DO WRONG HAS BEEN TAKEN AWAY!

(I Drink, smoke, do dope, play the lottery, dirty book/movies, chase women all I want to — I JUST DON"T WANT TO !)

THANK GOD.....I JUST DON'T WANT TO!
(Dwelling On The Mountain)

Would it be difficult to live a healthy life? Of course not! It is pleasant and easy to live life when you know that you are healthy and well! Is it difficult to live a *HOLY LIFE?* Of course not! Not if you have a **HOLY HEART** and a **MIND GIVEN OVER TO THE HOLY SPIRIT!**

HOLINESS is to the soul what **HEALTH** is to the body **SOUL NORMALCY.....!**

3. Holiness is SOUL SATISFACTION......!

Matt 5:6

Blessed are they which do hunger and thirst after righteousness: for they shall be filled. (KJV)

The blessedness does not consist in the *hungering or thirsting*.....**but rather in the FILLING!** HOLINESS implies **SATISFACTION WITH GOD** without the addition of anything else. It is like the man who is so in love with his wife and family and home that he doesn't feel the need or the urge to look at anybody or anywhere else.

Illus: Little boy named Charlie and his favorite aunt who always had a variety of fresh fruits. *CHARLIE WAS SATISFIED WITH APPLES !*

That is why one who has been truly **SANCTIFIED *wholly*** does not reach for the world or anything it offers but instead is enabled to live soberly, righteously and godly in this present world.

Titus 2:12
Teaching us that, denying ungodliness and worldly lusts, we ***should live soberly, righteously, and godly, in this present world;*** (KJV)

GOD'S WAY of keeping His people is not to keep them **FROM** temptation.....but rather to **KEEP THEM IN THE MIDST OF TEMPTATION!** God does not remove the world from their reach.....but gives them something better than the world has to offer! By doing this God nullifies the world's bid for their love and allegiance.

III. THE *INSISTENCE* OF HOLINESS......!

This premise is suggested by the initial word **"FOLLOW...."** in our Scripture lesson.

Heb 12:14
FOLLOW *peace with all men, and holiness, without which no man shall see the Lord: (KJV)*

This word translated follow in the Greek is the word:
dioko (dee-o'-ko); to pursue, follow (after), given to, (suffer)

persecute (-ion), press forward.

This word is a strong word. Its meaning, whether good or bad, depends upon the context....**BUT ALWAYS IT IS A STRONG WORD!** When it is used to describe opposition/persecution it is translated **"PERSECUTE"....**

Acts 22:4

And I **persecuted** *this way unto the death, binding and delivering into prisons both men and women. (KJV)*

When it is used to describe pursuit with intention to drive away, it is translated **"CHASE".** When it is used to describe pursuit with intention to apprehend it is translated **"PRESS".**

To "**FOLLOW HOLINESS**" can never mean simply not to oppose it, or to seek it half-heartedly! It **ALWAYS MEANS TO GO AFTER IT WITH ALL THE ZEAL YOU CAN MUSTER!** It is to desire it with such intense desire that all other desires become but weak wishes in comparison. It means to make real in the heart the saying:

"I would give all that I have to possess that experience.....!"

That is precisely what it will cost you to possess it!

Illus: Earl Jackson and his old fox hound, **"Trail "**. Trail by-passed the easier game, ignored the counterfeit, disregarded the smelly imitations, refused to be thrown off the track by his peers in the dog pack, plunging on through the briers and brambles, ignored the weather, swam the creeks, climbed the hillsides, refusing every call to quit until the prey was driven to ground. Sometimes Earl had to go back the next day to call "Old Trail" in.

This **HOLINESS** we are to pursue is a **DIVINE BESTOWAL** and it is within the reach of every man, woman, boy or girl who has been blood bought. Would you be honest with yourself and with God and answer the question:

"Do I possess such an experience in the Lord?"

If you cannot answer in the affirmative let me encourage you to ***FOLLOW AFTER IT*** until you indeed arrive at such an experience. Pursue it with zeal and courage and determination to possess it at any cost. This blessing is so important that you cannot see God WITHOUT IT!

— **HOLINESS IMPLIES FREEDOM FROM SIN.....**
— **HOLINESS IMPLIES SOUL NORMALCY....**
— **HOLINESS IMPLIES SOUL SATISFACTION...**

III John 5

Beloved, I wish above all things that thou mayest prosper and be in health, even as thy soul prospereth. (KJV)

Points To Ponder

1. Where does "holiness" originate?

____

1. What is the meaning of the word "holiness?"

____

3. What or Whom is the primary *(Vertical)* focus of holiness ? ______________________________________

4. What or Who is the secondary *(Horizontal)* focus of holiness ____________________________________

5. Define "imputation" in your own words.

____

____

____

6. Define "impartation" in your own words.

____

____

7. What are the three perspectives from which the subject of "Holiness" is approached?
1. _______________ 2. ________________
3. _______________

8 What is that one essential that one cannot see or approach God without ?

____

____

1. What is meant by the "Birth of the Spirit" ?

____

1. What is meant by the “Baptism of the Spirit? ?

Lesson Two

Holiness - It's Necessity

This is the second in a series of seven lessons in which we are going to consider together that great word found in the New Testament, ***Holiness*** or ***Sanctification***. The King James translates in the original autographs indiscriminately between these two words.

We shall consider in this lesson ***its necessity***, then in the next ***its nature***. Following that *its* ***way***, and then lesson five ***the time of its realization***.

1 Thess 4:1-4

1 Furthermore then we beseech you, brethren, and exhort you by the Lord Jesus, that as ye have received of us how ye ought to walk and to please God, so ye would abound more and more.

2 For ye know what commandments we gave you by the Lord Jesus.

3 **For this is the will of God , even your sanctification***, that ye should abstain from fornication:*

4 That every one of you should know how to possess his vessel in sanctification and honour;   KJV

There are two words in the New Testament relative to the state and position of the believer — ***Justification*** and ***Sanctification***. Bringing these two terms to their least common denominator we may say that:

— Justification means, ***"being counted righteous,"***

— Sanctification means, ***"being made righteous."*** When a man is ***Born Again***, God both **counts** him righteous, forgiving all the past — and **makes** him righteous giving him a new nature. This is initial sanctification. One can only be saved by and through the workings of the Holy Spirit. This is why Paul, when writing to the Christians of his day, though many of them were carnal ***(flesh driven)***, calls them saints, or sanctified ones.

Sanctification, however, is divided into two parts — ***"regeneration"*** or sanctification begun, and ***"sanctification entire"*** which is holiness accelerated. The purpose of this book is to explore the entire journey of holiness, to which we are focus our effort to walk therein.

Turn with me to Revelation 3: 14 – 22. Here the Lord, diagnosing the state of the Laodicean church, calls them *"Wretched, miserable, poor and blind and naked,"* finally He adds a most blessed promise,

Behold, I stand at the door and knock, if any man hear my voice and open the door, I will come in to him and will sup with him and he with me."

Notice if you will that those two do not come together; in between the description of the lukewarm Christian and the wonderful promise of an indwelling Christ, we have these words;

18 I counsel thee to buy of me gold tried in the fire, that thou mayest be rich; and white raiment, that thou mayest be clothed, and that the shame of thy nakedness do not appear; and anoint thine eyes with eyesalve, that thou mayest see. KJV

Then the writer adds:

20 **Behold, I** *stand at the door, and knock: if any man hear my voice, and open the door, I will come in to him, and* **will sup with him, and he with *me*.**

Here is the blessing; ***"Behold I.......will come in"*** even the Lord Jesus Christ Himself will enter to live within our hearts. For the Lord to indwell the heart that potential dwelling place must be pure and clean. That is reason enough for our seeking a holy heart in order that our Holy Lord would be pleased to live within! I want to present to you in this lesson the sevenfold necessity of being sanctified:

--- *1. Vision of Christ* ---

"Follow peace with all men,and holiness, **<u>without which no man shall see the Lord.</u>**" *Heb 12:14*

Let me give you the same verse of Scripture from the ***Amplified Bible:***

Heb 12:14

Strive to live in peace with everybody and **<u>pursue that consecration</u>** *and holiness without which no one will* **[ever]** *see the Lord. AMP*

This is the first reason for the work of sanctification to be done in our hearts. The necessity of having this work of grace to clear away the carnal *(human)* nature is — that without it we *"**<u>cannot</u>** see the Lord."*

— Matt 5:8 Blessed are the pure in heart: for they shall see God. KJV

While this primarily refers to the Lord's Return at the end of days, it also applies to us ***<u>here and now</u>***. The desire of every true child of God should be to see the Lord Jesus — we long for Him to be made manifest in our lives.

1 John 3:23-24

23 And this is his commandment, That we should believe on the name of his Son Jesus Christ, and love one another, as he gave us commandment.

24 **<u>And he that keepeth his commandments dwelleth in him, and he in him. And hereby we know that he abideth in us</u>**, *by the Spirit* which he hath given us. *KJV*

Have you ever thought about this in your study of the Word of God, the subject of seeing the Lord Jesus?

— ***The wise men*** when they saw the little Babe of Bethlehem knew it was the Lord! That knowledge led them to worship, adoration, and sacrificial giving.

— ***The Shepherds*** that came and saw the Babe, they knew Him! Their vision led to praise, thanksgiving, and testimony.

— ***The elderly man, Simeon***, the day that he came to the Temple had on many occasions seen babies in their mother's arms. But on this day, he saw Mary, just an ordinary peasant woman. He would have passed her by any other time, but being led of the Spirit, **he saw the Babe in her arms and he knew Him to be the Savior of the World !** He cried:

Luke 2:29-32

29 Lord, now lettest thou thy servant depart in peace, according to thy word:

30 **For mine eyes have seen thy salvation,**

31 Which thou hast prepared before the face of all people;

32 A light to lighten the Gentiles, and the glory of thy people Israel. KJV

— ***The prophetess, Anna***, who lived in the Temple came in later and she also, saw the young child and she knew it was the Christ. At once she begins to give thanks and spread it abroad for all to hear.

Luke 2:36-38

36 And there was one Anna , a prophetess, the daughter of Phanuel, of the tribe of Aser: she was of a great age, and had lived with an husband seven years from her virginity;

37 And she was a widow of about fourscore and four years, which departed

not from the temple, but served God with fastings and prayers night and day.

38 And she coming in that instant **gave thanks likewise**

unto the Lord, and spake of him to all them that looked for redemption in Jerusalem. *KJV*

— **The Samaritan woman** when she **saw Him** after she had received the life giving water in her soul knew Him to be her Savior. Her natural idea of a Messiah was of course that he would be a mighty king and national deliverer. But as soon as her heart was made pure she sees and believes that He that spoke unto her, was the "**ONE"!** Standing at her side, looking into her face, He brought salvation to her soul. This beatific *(blissful; saintly*) vision made her an instant missionary!

John 4:25-26

25 The woman saith unto him, I know that Messias cometh, which is called Christ: when he is come, he will tell us all things.

26 Jesus saith unto her, I that speak unto thee am he.

28 The woman then left her waterpot, and went her way into the city, and saith to the men,

29 **Come, see a man, which told me all things that ever I did: is not this the Christ?**

30 Then they went out of the city, and came unto him. KJV

That sanctifying fountain needs to baptize us that our eyes may be opened and ***we should go forth seeing the Lord*** — testifying to His grace, praising His name, telling the good tidings abroad, and made missionaries of the Cross.

We pass now to the next reason;

— 2. Oneness with Christ.....

John 17:17

Sanctify them through thy truth: thy word is truth.

21 That they all may be one ; as thou, Father, art in me, and I in thee, that they also may be one in us: that the world may believe that thou hast sent me.

22 And the glory which thou gavest me I have given them; that they may be one , even as we are one: KJV

Here is another of the deepest reasons for our being sanctified, that we may be one with the Lord! There is a self-evaluation that must take place, an honest, candid examination of our walk before the Lord. Listen to the Scriptures:

2 Tim 2:21

If a man **therefore purge himself** *from these, he shall be a vessel unto honour, sanctified, and meet for the master's use, and prepared unto every good work. KJV*

2 Cor 7:1

Having therefore these promises, dearly beloved, **let us cleanse ourselves** *from all filthiness of the flesh and spirit, perfecting holiness in the fear of God. KJV*

There is therefore a deeper purity and a closer union than some folks know anything about. In the epistle to the Romans we find the double union with Christ set forth clearly. In the sixth chapter the apostle speaks of a union with Christ in death, burial and resurrection, but in the seventh chapter he talks about a oneness with Christ in marriage, bringing forth fruit unto God.

He goes on to explain that there cannot be a oneness with Christ until the ***"old husband"*** is gone. What a picture of the carnal mind as the ***"old man"*** which is the ***"old husband"*** to whom we were married before Jesus came into our lives.

There can be no divorce, no suppression, no putting him down in the cellar or up in the attic. ***He has to die!*** Without his ***decease*** there can be ***no re-marriage*** and ***no oneness*** with Christ Jesus, the heavenly Bridegroom.

What we are after, is not some wonderful blessing that is going to make us independent of the Lord Jesus, but a blessing that will make us one with Him — one in desire, one in will, one in motive, one in God's desire for the salvation of a lost world, ***one with Christ.***

Salvation does not consist of ecstasies and emotions and talking in tongues. Rather it means I am brought into oneness with Christ, and if I am brought into this oneness with Christ it will make a tremendous difference in my life. I can look out on the world as Christ looks on it, and feel as **HE** feels, and love as **HE** loves, and walk as **HE** walked!

2. ***Usefulness and Power......*** *"If a man purge himself ...he shall be a vessel ..... sanctified and meet for the Master's use."* *2 Tim 2:21*

It is indeed a blessing to be one with Jesus, but there is a further reason that makes sanctification a necessity. It is expressed in the twenty-first verse we have just presented. We all know the miserable failures we are without the Lord on our side. Here is the reason why we lack power and are so needy to be usable in His service: we need a purging, a emptying out! Samuel Brengle, a great Salvationist soul, said, ***"Do not pray, Lord use me .....but, Lord make me usable!"***

God will use any man, woman, or young person to the utmost limit of their ability. So our effort should be to increase our abilities to be used of the Lord. When we get freed up from the twinge of envy, or even jealousy, that springs up in our hearts when we hear of some worker of the Lord being used more than we are, ***when we do not care who is used, only that the Lord Jesus is glorified*** — we are on the right road. Until we reach that inward purity, that absence of pride, of envy, of every evil work, until we are free of any and all of these, we are not meet for His use.

That is the reason why we need a clean heart. Then God can take us up as He pleases: He can put us down as He pleases, for He knows that we will not grumble or murmur, or complain, but will instead speak forth praise unto to His name. God has to do a deeper, more drastic work in our hearts than we dreamed of when we were in the land of Egypt ***(Sin)***. All we thought of when we were there was that we were in bondage! Now thank God we are out of bondage!

But when we get into the wilderness of our walk toward heaven and home, we are suddenly made to realize how much of Egypt there still lurks within us. No, we don't want to be there — nonetheless we find those things creeping into all that we do and say. That is why we begin the work of purging ourselves of the very last vestiges of the old Egyptian life and ways. Then we present our purged lives to the Lord for His use. How can the Lord Jesus take us and use us till He has made us **"every whit clean"** and free indeed in the whole.

There is yet another reason for our need of sanctification —

4. The Power to Love..... *"Seeing ye have PURIFIED your souls in obeying the truth ...... see that ye LOVE one another with a PURE heart fervently." (1 Peter 1:22)*

"The end of the commandment is LOVE out of a PURE heart." (! Tim 1:5)

Paul tells us that .... *"The kingdom of God is not meat and drink, but righteousness and peace and joy in the Holy Ghost." (Romans 14: 17)*

That is to say, it is not the meat and drink of the body which is needed, but it is the meat and drink of the soul. We might call righteousness, which is faith and love, ***the meat,*** while peace and joy are ***the drink*** of the soul.

There are a lot of people who are ***spiritual drunkards***: they want nothing but peace and joy, the more emotional experiences — but faith and love are not so much emotional as they are practical. The secret of the ability to love is a pure heart. Love to God and to man, pure and unadulterated, cannot proceed out of a heart that still has bitterness and envy lurking within.

Just as the fact that you cannot put the new wine of joy into old bottles, so you cannot put a patch of heavenly love on an old garment. The garments of holiness, the raiment of love is un-patched and unspotted and it is only in this condition that it can hide our nakedness and shame.

2 Tim 2:22

22 Flee also youthful lusts: but follow righteousness, faith, charity, peace, with them that call on the Lord out of a pure heart .

1 Peter 1:22

22 Seeing ye have purified your souls in obeying the truth through the Spirit unto unfeigned love of the brethren, see that ye love one another with a pure heart fervently: KJV

Can anything be more beautiful? Let us seek in these days with all our mind and soul and strength — and God will purify and fill us to the overflowing!

The Word presents us with yet another reason why we should be entirely sanctified:

5. Preparedness for the Lord's Coming ....

1 Thess 5:23-24

*23 And the very God of peace sanctify you **wholly** ; and I pray God your **whole spirit** and **soul** and **body** be preserved blameless unto the coming of our Lord Jesus Christ.*

24 **Faithful is he that calleth you, who also will do it.** *KJV*

Only the grace of God can make us right to be clothed with the white robes of the wedding garment, and the readiness for the Lord's appearing, and the right to enter the marriage supper of the

Lamb. These blessings have been purchased with our Savior's precious blood! **Glory!!!**

Here is a sixth reason:

6. The Ability to Praise in Time of Reproach.

Heb 13:12-15
12 Wherefore Jesus also, **that he might sanctify the people with his own blood, suffered without the gate.**
13 Let us go forth therefore unto him without the camp, bearing his reproach.
14 For here have we no continuing city, but we seek one to come.
15 By him therefore let us offer the sacrifice of praise to God continually, that is, the fruit of our lips giving thanks to his name. KJV

Pay close attention to the words, ***"Sanctify the people with His own blood...."*** . Some say that sanctification is the result of the Holy Spirit's indwelling us, and this is partially true, **but it is not the whole truth**. In Romans 5:9 we read that:

...being now **justified by his blood,** *we shall be saved from wrath through him. KJV*

But here in Hebrews we learn that His Blood sanctifies our hearts also. The meaning is clear. Before the Holy Ghost can come in and take possession, there has to be a purging of any and all things that this Holy Guest can move in and take possession. The point of the passage before us is that without His sanctifying power and grace we cannot **"go unto Him without the camp bearing His reproach."**

He sanctifies the people by His own blood in order that we might go without the camp, bearing His reproach. The body of the sin offering was burned outside the camp. It was entirely consumed, after certain parts had been burned upon the altar. The fire speaks to us of the Holy Ghost and the word **" body"** reminds us of the words of Paul – ***"The body of sin...."***

Rom 6:6

Knowing this, that our old man is crucified with him, that the body of sin might be destroyed, that henceforth we should not serve sin KJV

This language shows us that sin as a totality, an entity is destroyed and consumed. The blessed result will be that we shall have power to bear His reproach, and by Him offer the sacrifice of praise in the midst of persecution, obloquy*(ob-***block***'-y — censure, blame, or abusive language, discredit, disgrace)* and shame. Praise can never rise from a heart that is not purged and purified by His blood.

Finally, we present perhaps the most important result of a sanctified experience:

— 7. The Power to Obey....*1 Peter 1:2*

*Elect according to the foreknowledge of God the Father, through sanctification of the Spirit, __**unto obedience**__ and sprinkling of the blood of Jesus Christ: Grace unto you, and peace, be multiplied. KJV*

The heart of the Gospel of Jesus Christ is to make us obedient, even as the essence of sin made the human race disobedient. We are not only like lost sheep losing our way, ignorant of the way back, but we all have ***"gone our own way."*** Perhaps a very pleasant way, or a very respectable way, or even a good moral way, __*yet AWAY from God nevertheless!*__

The purpose of redemption is to bring us back to the place of perfect obedience. The Lord Jesus Himself came to show us its reasonableness, righteousness and blessedness by Himself living a life of unswerving obedience to the will of God. God the Holy Ghost can bring into captivity every thought to the obedience of

Christ. So, and only so, shall we gladly obey and follow in His steps.

What kind of people do we like to have around us? Is it not those who are faithful, gentle, kind, truthful, clean living, caring and obedient? What a comfort it is to be surrounded by such family, friends and acquaintances. Is God any different? By no means — He, too, does not want brilliant men and women so much as those who will be sanctified and become obedient servants.

Some of us know so well our own slip-shod nature; we may cover up and conceal it cleverly from our friends, but we know and God knows all about it. Thanks be to Him that He can alter and sanctify us body, soul and spirit, so that we obey Him and are at the ready for Him to use us for His glory.

I have placed before you some of the reasons why we need the great work of sanctification in our souls. Let us rehearse them again as we close this session.

(1) We need it that we may ***"see the Lord."*** Till the heart is pure there can be no vision: ***sin , fear and unbelief blur and dim the sight of our soul.***

Matt 5:8

Blessed are the pure in heart: for they shall see God.

Heb 12:14

Follow peace with all men, and holiness, without which no man shall see the Lord: KJV

(2) We need it that we may be one with Christ not only in will, but in desire and affection, mind and motive, yes, in all the powers and affections of our soul.

John 17:9-11

9 I pray for them: I pray not for the world, but for them which thou hast given me; for they are thine.

10 And all mine are thine, and thine are mine; and I am glorified in them.

11 And now I am no more in the world, but these are in the world, and I come to thee. Holy Father, keep through thine own name those whom thou hast given me, that they may be one, as we are. KJV

(3) We need it that we may be a vessel right for the Master's using. Power and usefulness are dependent on the sanctification of our nature.

2 Tim 2:21

If a man therefore purge himself from these, he shall be a vessel unto honour, sanctified, and meet for the master's use, and prepared unto every good work. KJV

(4) We need it that we can truly love. This cannot be until all evil has been drained from our heart. We cannot love till we are sanctified within — the pure essence of love can only be poured ***in*** and ***out*** of a clean vessel.

1 Peter 1:22

Seeing ye have purified your souls in obeying the truth through the Spirit unto unfeigned love of the brethren, see that ye love one another with a pure heart fervently: KJV *(Peter Lovest thou me.John 21)*

(5) We need it that we may be ready for Him at His appearing — that the shame of our nakedness may not appear.

Rev 3:18

I counsel thee to buy of me gold tried in the fire, that thou mayest be rich; and white raiment, that thou mayest be clothed, and ***that the shame of thy nakedness do not appear;*** KJV

(6) We need it that we may be enabled to bear His reproach without the camp and offer therein praise and thanksgiving.

Heb 13:15

By him therefore let us offer the sacrifice of praise to God continually, that is, the fruit of our lips giving thanks to his name KJV

(7) Finally, we need it that we may be perfectly obedient to our Master. Until all self-will and self-pleasing be taken out of our hearts we cannot follow in His steps.

1 Peter 1:2

Elect according to the foreknowledge of God the Father, through sanctification of the Spirit, unto obedience and sprinkling of the blood of Jesus Christ: Grace unto you, and peace, be multiplied. KJV

May the Holy Ghost make these thoughts a blessing to our souls and stir up our hearts to seek and to obtain all that is purchased and procured for us through the sacrifice of our caring Lord. ***Amen!***

Points To Ponder

1. Explain the biblical meaning of Justification and of Sanctification____________________________________

2. Why is a Vision of Christ essential to the pursuit of holiness?____________________________________

3. What is meant by "oneness" with Christ ?

4. Explain the "Power of Love".

5. Explain the "Power of Praise".

6. Explain the "Power of Obedience".

7. What are we to be *"prepared" for and "looking"* for in our day to day living? ____________________________________

Lesson Three

Holiness – It's Nature

Our study now takes us into the consideration of the nature of this great experience described in the Word of God as ***Sanctification*** or the ***State of Holiness of Heart***. It may be defined as righteousness ***imparted*** **(to give/bestow)** just as justification may be called righteousness ***imputed*** **(to attribute/ascribe)**. This is

"THE holiness* (sanctification) *without which no man shall see the Lord." (Heb 12:4)

The faculties, of the human soul may be described as follows, ***Conscience, Will, Mind, Memory, Imagination, Affections*** and ***Desires.*** All of these are constituent elements of our human nature. We are all conscious of these faculties inside of us and their activity: and we are all equally conscious, ***if we but think about it,*** that every one of them has been distorted, perverted, poisoned and rendered ineffective by the work of the enemy of the soul.

Therefore, it may be helpful to consider what is done in the various faculties of our nature, taking them one by one — and finally to investigate the cause and root of all the trouble they cause the unsanctified individual. Above all I would want you to be convinced that ***God desires to purify all these faculties and powers***, so that everything within would be a blessing to His holy name. ***Is this possible, or is it too good to be true?*** Surely not with such a God as our God, and with such a Saviour as our Saviour, the Lord Jesus Christ. First then we consider:

1. **The Conscience.....**

Heb 9:14

How much more shall the blood of Christ, who through the

eternal Spirit offered himself without spot to God, **purge your conscience** *from dead works to serve the living God? KJV*

When we were sinners we sought and found the pardon for our sins, the clamor of our awakened conscience was stilled by the blood of Jesus which silences its fierce accusations and its sting*(er)* is extracted and the clamor is silenced.

But there is an even greater change that takes place — **the Conscience is renewed!** Some of the vilest of unregenerate men and women have been made to become the most tender and conscientious, as their consciences have become enlightened and renewed.

But our text, speaks of a yet deeper experience, *"purified from dead works"* to serve the living God. Not merely freed from past sin and guilt, nor from misguided or mistaken zeal — ***but from doing things in our own strength***. The conscience is cleansed and purified; and it is the blood of Jesus that does the work.

The allusion in our text is to the sprinkling of water containing the ashes of the red heifer, upon the priests, who had been engaged in burying the bodies of the dead that had been slain by the plague. Instead of serving in prayer and praise and worship in the Holy Place which was their normal realm of responsibility, they were engaged in this burial task.

So shall it be with our conscience when we claim as our own the blessed cleansing of the blood of Jesus in all its fullness. Then ***we shall wait on God*** who waits to work in us — to work through us, and to work for us!

2. The Will.......

The Will is the *citadel of the soul!* It is often called the ***"ego"*** *(Acronym* – Edging God Out), the very self of man. Until this is surrendered — captured — harnessed — there is nothing for God accomplished. When we are ***Born Again*** of His Spirit, it is then God's Holy Spirit and grace can begin to work within the believer so that the will is transformed, the ego is surrendered to the Lord.

The work is begun at Calvary through the sacrifice of the all-cleansing, all-empowering blood of the Lamb. In the surrender of ***"sanctification"*** the gift of our selves ***(ego included)*** is proffered to God and there the ***"citadel falls"*** in total submission to its new ***"Lord and Master."***

This presentation is not an arrival – ***rather it is a departure!*** Many suppose that the surrender of the will is all. If we buy into that premise it will not be long before we discover our mistake. When the devil did his work of sin in our lives, he did a thorough job of it. Every part of our nature was twisted, perverted, poisoned by his soul killing virus.

Sanctification is the antidote for Satan's malady. God, through the workings and leading of the Holy Spirit, begins bringing a perfect cure and thoroughly sets about the task of undoing all that the devil has wrought within. This is an on-going process that continues after we have made the initial presentation of ourselves to God as ***"living sacrifices."*** As things are revealed to us and brought into focus through our continued surrender and obedience to the ***"Will of God"*** the sanctification continues.

Strictly speaking, our **conscience** and **will** are ***the two great spheres of our nature*** in which God's regenerating grace operates. Sin caused the soul of man to ***degenerate*** and it is the ***New Birth*** and the ***Sanctification*** of the Holy Spirit that ***regenerates*** the soul of man.

— Our conscience is ***"purified"***

Heb 9:14

How much more shall the blood of Christ, who through the eternal Spirit offered himself without spot to God, ***purge your***

conscience from dead works *to serve the living God? KJV*

— Our will is ***"crucified"***

Gal 2:20

I am crucified with Christ: nevertheless I live; yet not I, but Christ liveth in me*: and the life which I now live in the flesh I live by the faith of the Son of God, who loved me, and gave himself for me. KJV*

But sanctification entire and complete covers wider and deeper ground than these:

3. The Desires...

"They that are Christ's have crucified the flesh WITH the affections and lusts." (Gal. 5:24)

The wider and deeper ground I referred to is the ***desires*** of the heart. In the Hebrew and Greek original autographs of the Scripture, there are some sixteen words used to express the noun. In twenty six such instances the verb ***"desire"*** is used. Sanctification reaches these deep places of the soul.

John Wesley stated on one occasion **"My will seems fixed, yet wide my passions rove...."** Oh, brothers/sisters how we need to guard our hearts! Our conscience, that which is deeper down in the soul than our wills are, entertain ***"desires"***. Desires so strong that they can bring again into captivity the will that has been set free.

How do we guard against inordinate desires? Here is the answer in a nut-shell — ***"Desire Nothing But God!"*** Are our desires fixed like the Psalmist?

Ps 57:7

My heart is fixed , O God, **my heart is fixed** *: I will sing* *and give praise.*

Ps 112:7
He shall not be afraid of evil tidings: **his heart is fixed** *, trusting in the LORD. KJV*

— Isaiah tells us that our minds must be stayed or fixed on God.

Isa 26:3
Thou wilt keep him in perfect peace, ***whose mind is stayed on thee****: because he trusteth in thee. KJV*

The Holy Spirit uses a stronger word — ***"Crucifixion."***

Gal 5:24
And they that are Christ's have crucified the flesh with the affections and lusts. KJV

Our worldly and carnal desires can be nailed to the Cross !

4. The Affections ....

Deut 30:6
And the LORD thy God will circumcise thine heart, ... to love the LORD thy God with all thine heart, and with all thy soul, that thou mayest live. KJV

There is one command — the greatest — more beautiful than all the others:

Deut 6:
4 Hear, O Israel: The LORD our God is one LORD:
5 ***And thou shalt love the LORD thy God with all thine heart, and with all thy soul, and with all thy might.***

Mark 12:
29 ....The first of all the commandments is, Hear, O

Israel; The Lord our God is one Lord:

30 **<u>And thou shalt love the Lord thy God with all thy heart, and with all thy soul, and with all thy mind, and with all thy strength: this is the first commandment.</u>**

31 And the second is like, namely this, Thou shalt love thy neighbour as thyself. There is none other commandment greater than these. KJV

There is a promise, too, more comforting and precious — the one that I opened this section with ..... *"The Lord thy God will CIRCUMCISE thine heart to LOVE........"* What makes this command so beautiful? It is not *"thou shalt serve..."* nor *"thou shalt worship...."* nor *"thou shalt obey...."* — it is ***<u>"thou shalt love.....!"</u>***

No man asks a woman to love him unless he has first expressed that he loves her! Such is the case too, with God. He could not bid us to love Him with all our heart, if He had not first loved us!

1 John 4:

17 Herein is our love made perfect, that we may have boldness in the day of judgment: because as he is, so are we in this world.

18 There is no fear in love; but perfect love casteth out fear: because fear hath torment. He that feareth is not made perfect in love.

19 **<u>We love him, because he first loved us .</u>** *KJV*

Why is faithfulness and devotion to God so difficult with some people? The reason is simple, **<u>they are not in love with Him.</u>**

Let me explain it this way: A young man has a job and he has to travel fifteen miles to the job and fifteen miles back. In all kinds of weather, rain, snow, sunshine, hot and cold, night time and the wee hours of the morning. He grumbles and murmurs and complains. Then one day he meets a girl that lives close to his job and he falls in love with her.

Suddenly the same road he has complained about becomes an easy trip and he delights to travel it. He leaves early for work and stops by after work. There is no more complaining, no more grumbling — why? **Love has made the difference!** So it will be when our hearts are circumcised to love the Lord!

Paul uses the word circumcised in regard to our ***"sanctification"***.

Col 2:11
*In whom also ye are circumcised with the circumcision made without hands, **in putting off the body of the sins of the flesh by the circumcision of Christ:*** *KJV*

The inference is of putting away ***the whole body*** as opposed to the part taken away in the physical act of circumcision. It is a blessed taking away from and out of us, all that deflects our love and would hinder our ***whole-hearted*** devotion to the Lord that we love and now follow!

5. The Imagination.......

Gen 6:5
*And GOD saw that the wickedness of man was great in the earth, **and that every imagination of the thoughts of his heart was only evil continually.*** *KJV*

The subject of the imagination in the Scriptures is broad. The prophet Jeremiah speaks of the imagination in the context of it being followed and trusted and obeyed rather than God's Word.

Jer 7:24
*But they hearkened not, nor inclined their ear, **but walked in the counsels and in the imagination of their evil heart, and went backward, and not forward.*** *KJV*

There are eight references to the ***"imagination"*** in Jeremiah's writings and there are three distinct words in the Old Testament which are all translated ***"Imagination."*** The first means ***"Formation,"*** the second ***"Device,"*** and the third means ***"Stubbornness."*** Jeremiah uniformly employs the last – man's "**Stubbornness!**"

We could very well say that the imagination, *that faculty that is always forming and giving shape to things that do not exist,* is the stronghold of unbelief.

— We imagine that God is hard and austere;
— We imagine His way is difficult;
— We imagine His will is unbearable;
— We imagine that God is unreasonable;
— We imagine trouble that never materializes;
— We imagine difficulties that never appear.

This is all the work of unbelief. Unbelief says *"it can't be done"*, it's *"too good to be true"*! Unbelief whispers that sin is too strong, the giants are too big, the circumstances too difficult, the price too high. Unbelief paints upon the screen of imagination fearful specters of failure and catastrophes! These are all the poison of unbelief ! The heart will never be established or fixed until the imagination of man is cleansed, and then stayed upon God as Isaiah declares,

Isa 26:3
Thou wilt keep him in perfect peace , whose mind (Imagination) is stayed on thee: because he trusteth in thee. KJV

Guard against ***"forming"*** a god of your own making — one made after your own likeness, the outcome of a diseased imagination, saturated with the poison of unbelief. ***God can, and must, sanctify even our imaginations and cast out all unbelief***, so that we shall walk not according to the imagination of our own carnal heart but according to His "**law**," His "**voice**," and His "**word**."

6. The Mind ....

Eph 4:22-24

22 That ye put off concerning the former conversation the old man, which is corrupt according to the deceitful lusts;

23 **And be renewed in the spirit of your mind;**

24 And that ye put on the new man, which after God is created in righteousness and true holiness. KJV

In speaking of the mind reference is to the thought of the heart. Some seem to think that God cannot deal with our thoughts, and yet —

Prov 23:7

For as he thinketh in his heart, so is he: KJV

— Sow a thought — you reap an act;
— Sow an act and you reap a habit;
— Sow a habit, you reap a character;
— Sow a character and your reap a destiny.

How true that the thinking of our heart are most important. I know that ***desire, imagination,*** and ***will*** are all elemental in the construction of our thoughts — but for the sake of clarity I believe that the ***"cleansing of the thoughts of the heart by the inspiration of the Holy Spirit"*** falls into a category of its own.

There are ***"thoughts of evil"*** passing through our minds, they come in for a moment and are gone almost as quickly — leaving no stain, no guilt, no sting or aftermath of pain. I am not speaking about these.

But, there are ***"evil thoughts"***, these arise from the heart and mar and scar; blister and burn; and will carry us into captivity. They will fix and make our character if not attended to. Is there a balm in Gilead? Is there a remedy? The blood of Jesus Christ not only brings pardon, but cleanses and removes the evil — purifying the fountainhead of our spirit by the ***"renewing*** **in the spirit** ***of***

our mind." When we present the man God can

"bring into captivity every thought to the obedience of Christ." 2 Cor 10:5

— 7. The Memory ....

2 Peter 3:1

This second epistle, beloved, I now write unto you; in both which I ***stir up your pure minds by way of remembrance:*** *KJV*

Probably there is no part of our nature that reveals the evil effects of the fall of man more than our diseased memory. Why is it that we find it so easy to remember the sad and bad yet forget the good? Moses in his closing charge to the Israelites stressed it again and again – remember, remember, remember!

— Remember the bond-service in Egypt!

Deut 24:22

And thou shalt remember that thou wast a bondman in the land of Egypt: therefore I command thee to do this thing.

— Remember the sin in the wilderness.....

Deut 9:7

Remember, and forget not, how thou provokedst the LORD thy God to wrath in the wilderness: from the day that thou didst depart out of the land of Egypt, until ye came unto this place, ye have been rebellious against the LORD.

— Remember the judgment on Pharaoh.....

Deut 7:18

Thou shalt not be afraid of them: but shalt well remember what the LORD thy God did unto Pharaoh, and unto all Egypt;

— Remember that God is the Giver of ALL things ...

Deut 8:18

But thou shalt remember the LORD thy God: for it is he that giveth thee power to get wealth, that he may establish his covenant which he sware unto thy fathers, as it is this day.

— Remember the day of your Exodus .....

Ex 16:1-2

1 And they took their journey from Elim, and all the congregation of the children of Israel came unto the wilderness of Sin, which is between Elim and Sinai, on the fifteenth day of the second month after their departing out of the land of Egypt.

2 And the whole congregation of the children of Israel murmured against Moses and Aaron in the wilderness:

— Remember God's judgment of Miriam .....

Deut 24:9

Remember what the LORD thy God did unto Miriam by the way, after that ye were come forth out of Egypt.

— Remember the hindering Amalek .....

Deut 25:17-18

17 Remember what Amalek did unto thee by the way, when ye were come forth out of Egypt;

18 How he met thee by the way, and smote the hindmost of thee, even all that were feeble behind thee, when thou wast faint and weary; and he feared not God.

— Remember the Sabbath .....

Ex 20:8

Remember the sabbath day, to keep it holy.

Peter also wrote to believers of remembrance.....

2 Peter 3:1

This second epistle, beloved, I now write unto you; in both which I stir up your pure minds by way of remembrance:

How fickle and foolish is our memory! There are only three things that can change it, heal it, and keep it fresh:

— The Word of God
— The Spirit of God
— The Blood of Jesus!

John 16:4

But these things have I told you, that when the time shall come, ye may remember that I told you of them. **(The WORD of God)**

John 14:26

But the Comforter, which is the Holy Ghost, whom the Father will send in my name, he shall teach you all things, and bring all things to your remembrance, whatsoever I have said unto you. **(The SPIRIT of God)**

Luke 22:19-20

19 And he took bread, and gave thanks, and brake it, and gave unto them, saying, This is my body which is given for you: this do in remembrance of me.

20 Likewise also the cup after supper, saying, This cup is the new testament in my blood, which is shed for you. KJV
(The BLOOD of God)

How can we remember unless we read and meditate on His Word? How can we remember unless the blessed Holy Spirit is our **"Divine Remembrancer"** ? How shall He keep us in remembrance unless the blood has first been applied to heal and cleanse?

Such is the sevenfold work of Sanctification. Our ***Conscience*** purified from dead works and renewed. Our ***Will*** transfigured. Our ***Affections*** circumcised. Our ***Desires*** nailed to the Cross. Our ***Mind*** renewed in its spirit. Our ***Imagination*** stayed/fixed on God. Our ***Memory*** healed.

God has appointed to utter destruction ***"the man of sin"*** within our hearts. Let our cry be ***"Crucify him!" "Away with him!"*** Let none of Achan's spirit lurk within our breast.

Instead let us see Jesus lifted up as the serpent and made a curse for us — then let us bow in faith and worship, praising Him till we find in blessed experience that **ALL the evil is cast out;** our hearts purified, and that everything within us does bless His Holy Name.

Points To Ponder

1. Justification may be called righteousness
____ ?

2. Sanctification may be called righteousness
____?

3. The faculties of the human soul are ____________,
____________, ______________, ________________,
____________, ______________, ________________?

1. What has the enemy of man's soul done to all of these faculties ?________________________________
____

1. What does God desire to do to each of these faculties of man ? _____________________________________
____
____

6. What must be done to the conscience of man ?
____

7. The will is called "the ______________________ of the ___________________________" ?

8. What is the acronym for the word "ego" ?
____

1. What must be done to the "desires" and "affections" in sanctification ? _____________________________
____

1. Explain the difference between an "evil thought" and "thoughts of evil". ______________________________
____

11. Is an “evil thought” sinful, staining the soul ?

12. What is the end result of “thoughts of evil” ?

Lesson Four

Holiness – It's Way

1 Thess 5:23-24

23 And the very God of peace sanctify you wholly*; and I pray God your* ***whole spirit*** *and* ***soul*** *and* ***body*** *be preserved blameless unto the coming of our Lord Jesus Christ.*

24 Faithful is he that calleth you, who also will do it. KJV

In this fourth lesson we begin to consider the **WAY** that God takes in purifying the heart. So far we have thought of the ***necessity*** and ***nature*** of this great work of the Holy Spirit. May that same blessed Spirit direct our hearts down this avenue of discovery!

— 1. God Himself Does it by LOVE

God answers man's query ***"how"*** with a gift. Nicodemus asked, *"How can a man be born again?"* The woman at the well asked *"How can you get the living water seeing the well is deep?"* The disciples asked, *"How can we eat Thy flesh and drink Thy blood?"* They asked, *"How wilt Thou manifest Thyself to us and not unto the world?"* They asked, *"How are the dead raised up?"*

To all of these enquires the Lord replies — It is the gift of God!

John 3:16

For God so loved the world, that ***he gave his only begotten Son****, that whosoever believeth in him should not perish, but have everlasting life. KJV*

He so loved that He **"GAVE"!**

"I will ***GIVE*** *you Living Water." "I will* ***GIVE*** *my flesh and blood for the life of the world." "I will* ***GIVE*** *you another Comforter." "Thou fool, God* ***GIVETH*** *it a body."*

And such is the case with the experience of sanctification that we have under consideration at this time. It is a gift — ! ***A gift is a gift! Repentance***, ***Faith***, and ***Consecration*** are all man's part — but **Sanctification is a gift** — something that God does ***in us*** and ***for us!***

John Wesley was asked once WHEN one should preach the doctrine of entire sanctification? To this question he replied;

"Never until men are **hungry** ***and*** **seeking** ***for it, and then when you do, let it always be by drawing rather than by driving."***

The Lord Jesus in dealing with men and women always approached them in such a way that of their own accord they confessed their sin and need.

He draws you now. He calls you now. He tells you that it is **HE**, ***Himself*** who does the work, the very ***God of Peace Himself.***

— *2. By Chastening*

Heb 12:9-10
9 Furthermore we have had fathers of our flesh which corrected us, and we gave them reverence: shall we not much rather be in subjection unto the Father of spirits, and live?
10 For they verily for a few days chastened us after their own pleasure; ***but he for our profit, that we might be partakers of his holiness.***

In this twelfth chapter of the Epistle to the Hebrews, if you read it carefully, you will notice the word ***"endurance"***.

In verse one it is translated ***"patience":***

hupomone *(hoop-om-on-**ay'**); cheerful (or hopeful) endurance, constancy: - enduring, patience, patient continuance (waiting).*

In verses two, three, and seven it is translated ***"endure, endurance, endured"*** — ***huios*** — *(hwee-os'); apparently a primary* word; a "son" (sometimes of animals), used very widely of immediate, remote or figuratively, kinship: KJV - child, foal, son.

Our wonderful Lord endured two things, ***the Cross***, and the ***contradiction of sinners***. If Jesus could endure the ridicule and the rancor of sinners, then how much more should we, the sinners He died to save, endure patiently the chastening and the rebuke of our heavenly Father?

There can be no sanctifying grace without this. Are we prepared for His convicting, chastening Word? Without conviction for holiness we can get nowhere.

Heb 12:10

*For they verily for a few days chastened us after their own pleasure; but he for our profit, that we might be partakers of **his holiness.** KJV*

The word ***"holiness"*** here in verse ten is ***hagiotes*** (hag-ee-**ot'**-ace); sanctity ***(i.e. properly, the state of holiness).***

In verse fourteen it is ***hagiasmos*** (hag-ee-as-**mos'**); **properly, purification, i.e. (the state) purity; concretely a purifier:**

The first speaks of a *state,* the last speaks of a *process* – bringing us into that state. How wonderful is the divine inspiration of the Word of God. The verbal inspiration, the very words — nouns and verbs and adjectives — are all used with such precision and exactness to deliver the deep meaning from the heart of God.

When the Spirit of truth first visits our hearts He reproves and rebukes us making us miserable. His chastening hand brings us to the place of our seeking to move closer to Him. God wants us to be partakers of His holy nature. He invites you, draws you, allures you, and in tenderness chastens you that you may be ***"sanctified"*** and meet for the Master's use.

Don't be afraid of it. Don't run away from it. You will never get this blessing by understanding the doctrine, or by study and by knowing all about its philosophy. You cannot get in ***"head first."*** It is a matter of the ***"heart"*** and bowing before God's chastening, convicting hand. In doing so you enter in.

— 3. By the Promises

2 Cor 7:1-2

Having therefore these promises, dearly beloved, let us cleanse ourselves *from all filthiness of the flesh and spirit,* ***perfecting holiness in the fear of God.***

2 Peter 1:4

Whereby are **given unto us exceeding great and precious promises: that by these ye might be partakers of the divine nature, having escaped the corruption that is in the world through lust. KJV**

What is the ***"Divine nature"***? ***"God is a Spirit." "God is light." "God is love." "God is a consuming fire."*** This is the fourfold definition of God's nature set forth in the New Testament Scriptures.

John 4:24

God is a Spirit *: and they that worship him must worship him in spirit and in truth.*

1 John 1:5

This then is the message which we have heard of him, and declare unto you, that ***God is light ,*** *and in him is no darkness at all.*

1 John 4:8

He that loveth not knoweth not God; for ***God is love*** *.*

Heb 12:29

For our ***God is a consuming fire .***

All of this is for us through the blessed promises of God. These are what convey to us the blessing. I know of no one entering the blessed state of sanctification other than through the promises of God.

As seekers we need to get alone, and read and re-read, affirm and re-affirm, plead and plead again, the great and precious promises before the Lord. In doing so the fountain of faith will spring up in our hearts and will enable us to believe that the work is done.

There is only one way to wrest the devil's weapons from him. The written word alone prevails — ***"Thus saith the Lord.....!"***. The Lord Jesus in the Wilderness used it in this fashion. The words He quoted were from the Book of Deuteronomy and were all selected from the story of His people in the Wilderness.

Jesus, Himself, tempted there in the desert wilderness, puts Himself back with His people in that same position. He meets the enemy with words of victory where they had met defeat.

Deut 8:3

And he humbled thee, and suffered thee to hunger, and fed thee with manna, which thou knewest not, neither did thy fathers know; **that he might make thee know that man doth not live by bread only, but by every word that proceedeth**

out of the mouth of the LORD doth man live.

Luke 4:3-4

3 And the devil said unto him, If thou be the Son of God, command this stone that it be made bread.

4 And Jesus answered him, saying, It is written, ***That man shall not live by bread alone , but by every word of God.***

Deut 6:16

Ye shall not tempt the LORD your God, *as ye tempted him in Massah.*

Matt 4:5-7

5 Then the devil taketh him up into the holy city, and setteth him on a pinnacle of the temple,

6 And saith unto him, If thou be the Son of God, cast thyself down: for it is written, He shall give his angels charge concerning thee: and in their hands they shall bear thee up, lest at any time thou dash thy foot against a stone.

7 Jesus said unto him, It is written again, **Thou shalt not tempt the Lord *thy God.*** *KJV*

Deut 5:6-9

6 I am the LORD thy God , which brought thee out of the land of Egypt, from the house of bondage.

7 **Thou shalt have none other gods before me.**

8 Thou shalt not make thee any graven image, or any likeness of any thing that is in heaven above, or that is in the earth beneath, or that is in the waters beneath the earth:

9 **Thou shalt not bow down thyself unto them, nor serve them: for I the LORD thy God**

Matt 4:8-10

8 Again, the devil taketh him up into an exceeding high mountain, and sheweth him all the kingdoms of the world, and the glory of them;

9 And saith unto him, All these things will I give thee, if thou wilt fall down and worship me.

10 Then saith Jesus unto him, Get thee hence, Satan: **for**

it is written, Thou shalt worship the Lord thy God, and him only shalt thou serve. *KJV*

God sanctifies us through His promises. Through them He draws, encourages, chastens, convicts, and lovingly offers us His exceeding great and precious promises. Grab hold with all your might the things that are promised — ***sanctification entire being one of them!***

1 Thess 4:3

For this is the will of God, even your sanctification, ... KJV

— 4. By the Blood of Jesus......

Heb 13:12

Wherefore Jesus also, that he might sanctify the people with his own blood, *suffered without the gate. KJV*

Here is the crux of the whole matter — the cause of the great transaction. In Romans 5:9 we learn that we :

.....being **now justified by his blood,** *we shall be saved from wrath through him. KJV*

But this passage from the Scriptures tells us deeper things — it tells us we are ***"Sanctified by the Blood."*** It is because of this that many miss the blessing of sanctification because they never see the Cross of Christ as the means of their sanctification. That He died for their sins they know well, but that He died ***"to put away sin"*** is hidden from their eyes.

They have seen Him as the Lamb of God who died in their stead on behalf of their transgressions — but they have never beheld Him lifted up as the Serpent — made a curse on their behalf — to take away their sin and cleans all the ***old serpent virus*** from their nature.

The apostle Paul speaks of the Cross – John tells of the blood – Peter seeks to show us the stripes and the sufferings of the Saviour – to make us ***"free"*** and ***"clean"*** and ***"whole."*** The mystery of it all we may never fully understand, but faith believes and appropriates **ALL** that His death has secured for our sanctification.

Over fifty years ago I was saved by the blood of Jesus and its merits canceled the sin debt which I owed, but to-day at this very moment, what is it doing for me in its practical working?

The apostle John gives us four blessings secured for those that eat His flesh and drink His blood.

– First – The gift of eternal life. ***Here is feeding on Him as the Passover Lamb.***

– Second – An indwelling Christ. ***Here is a partaking of His sacrifice as the Peace Offering.***

– Third – The power to serve. ***Here is feeding upon the Sin Offering on others' behalf.***

– Fourth – A future and everlasting salvation – ***eating of Christ as the Trespass Offering.***

John 6

44 No man can come to me, except the Father which hath sent me draw him: and I will raise him up at the last day.

45 It is written in the prophets, And they shall be all taught of God. Every man therefore that hath heard, and hath learned of the Father, cometh unto me.

46 Not that any man hath seen the Father, save he which is of God, he hath seen the Father.

47 Verily, verily, I say unto you, He that believeth on me hath everlasting life.

48 I am that bread of life.

49 Your fathers did eat manna in the wilderness, and are dead.

50 This is the bread which cometh down from heaven, that a man may eat thereof, and not die.

51 I am the living bread which came down from heaven: if

any man eat of this bread, he shall live for ever: and the bread that I will give is my flesh, which I will give for the life of the world.

52 The Jews therefore strove among themselves, saying, How can this man give us his flesh to eat?

53 Then Jesus said unto them, Verily, verily, I say unto you, Except ye eat the flesh of the Son of man, and drink his blood, ye have no life in you.

54 Whoso eateth my flesh, and drinketh my blood, hath eternal life; and I will raise him up at the last day.

55 For my flesh is meat indeed, and my blood is drink indeed.

56 He that eateth my flesh, and drinketh my blood, dwelleth in me, and I in him.

57 As the living Father hath sent me, and I live by the Father: so he that eateth me, even he shall live by me.

58 This is that bread which came down from heaven: not as your fathers did eat manna, and are dead: he that eateth of this bread shall live for ever.

59 These things said he in the synagogue, as he taught in Capernaum. KJV

We must learn well the lesson that the Holy Ghost can never enter to abide within us except on one ground, ***the sacrifice of the Slain Lamb.*** No tears or prayers, no repentance or vows of consecration, no works of obedience will ever ensure His indwelling. He can only enter our hearts as an ***Abiding Guest*** in response to faith in the Blood of Jesus.

We are sanctified and made clean by ***His*** blood, not by our tears. We are crucified with ***Him*** through His cross, and not by our own sufferings and mortification. Our fallen, diseased nature is made whole by ***His*** stripes, not by any efforts or vows of consecration of our own.

If all the imaginations of all men who have ever lived were rolled into one, they could never fathom the mystery or understand what it meant for the holy, sinless, spotless Son of God — *who had never experienced a sinful thought, an angry temper, a jealous feeling, a lustful desire* — to have the ocean this world's vile, unthinkable, unspeakable filthiness by fallen man to surge over His spotless soul?

We cannot understand; but we can believe that He Is Able to sanctify us with His Blood. When our mind wraps around that glorious fact then the soul finds a rock beneath its feet that can cause us to have a power and confidence that cannot be shaken. When you know and feel that you are made ***HOLY by His blood*** all pride in self-effort falls away.

The theory that the Holy Spirit enters our hearts the moment we are saved and keeps us from ever yielding to sin is woefully inadequate. Before this takes place there has to be a ***definite, instantaneous*** and ***radical adjustment of our soul!*** A presentation and a purifying of the secret springs of our being from the nature of our natural father, Adam — and then an in-filling of the Spirit of our heavenly Father to keep us moment by moment from yielding to the temptations of the tempter.

This sin-destroying, sanctifying experience is effected by His shedding of His blood upon the Cross and apprehended by the living faith of an humbled soul and maintained moment by moment by a total abandonment and obedience to the Lord of our life.

– 5. By the Spirit –

1 Peter 1:2

Elect according to the foreknowledge of God the Father, **through sanctification of the Spirit**, *unto obedience and sprinkling of the blood of Jesus Christ: KJV*

The fullness of the divine triune God head is involved in this work within the life of the believer. ***God the Father***, by His calling, chastening, promising love does the work. ***The Lord Jesus***, by His death and shedding of blood procures and provides this divine gift. ***The Holy Ghost*** is the one who takes up His abode in the cleansed, purged, and purified heart.

"It is expedient," said Jesus, *"that I go away for if I go not away the Comforter will not come unto you, but if I depart, I will send Him unto you." (John 6:7)*

If the Saviour had remained on earth, how few of us would have seen Him — every train, plane, ship, and highway would have been crowded with pilgrims the world over to see Jesus. How few, comparatively speaking, of the poor would ever have had a glimpse of His face.

But the Comforter has come that all may see the Lord. It is He that takes the things of Christ and shows them to us. How can the blood of Jesus, shed better than two millenniums ago, cleanse my soul from sin? How can my inner selfish nature be crucified and purged of self with a Christ nailed to the Cross so long ago? How can my memory and my mind and will be made whole by the lacerated body of Christ on the Cross? To all these questions the Saviour replies:

John 14:26
But the Comforter , which is the Holy Ghost, whom the Father will send in my name, he shall teach you all things, and bring all things to your remembrance, whatsoever I have said unto you.

John 16:7
Nevertheless I tell you the truth; It is expedient for you that I go away: for if I go not away, the Comforter will not come unto you; **but if I depart, I will send him unto you.** *KJV*

Only the Holy Ghost can show us the way and only the Holy Ghost can bring us in. If the Lord Jesus had to offer Himself through the eternal Spirit, how much more are we dependent upon His constraining, compelling, enlightening, enabling power.

As we await then upon God, pleading the promises, knowing our own impotence — let us remember He is there to help us. To help us believe, and bring every thought into captivity to the obedience of Christ.

— 6. *By the Word.......*

Mark 1:42

And as soon as he had spoken, immediately the leprosy departed from him, and he was cleansed.

John 15:3

Now ye are clean through the word which I have spoken unto you. KJV

This is our final consideration for this session — we have seen that God gives us and uses His promises to effect the sanctification of our hearts. We can only really believe God, the finished work of Christ, and the operating presence of the Holy Ghost ***through the written Word.***

By hiding the promises of God given in His Word within our minds and hearts, and appropriating them as ours, and using them against the attacks of the devil we can be victorious. Still after we have done this by stepping out on His promises, burning our bridges behind us, — God still has a further work to do through His Word. By it He seals His own work. The Scriptures provide us with repeated instances of His working through His Word to accomplish His agenda.

— **Isaiah 6:7** — There we see that after the live coal had touched his lips and he had felt the burning cleansing flame, the seraphim spake saying,

"........Lo, this hath touched thy lips; and thine iniquity is taken away, and thy sin purged. KJV

— **Mark 5:29** — The Lord stayed her steps, and gave her a word of sealing to her soul. *"Thy* **faith** *hath made thee whole,..."* Not her prayer, not her decision, not her consecration, not her earnestness, not her zeal, not her feeling, but by simply believing she was restored.

Mark 5:29

And straightway the fountain of her blood was dried up; and she felt in her body that she was healed of that plague. KJV

— **Mark 1:40,41** — The leper had sought the Lord in despair and yet in faith he had believed. The Lord was moved with compassion, stretched forth His hand and touched him. Neither the touch nor the compassion accomplished the cure — but as soon as He had **spoken** the work was done.

40 And there came a leper to him, beseeching him, and kneeling down to him, and saying unto him, If thou wilt, thou canst make me clean.

41 And Jesus, moved with compassion, put forth his hand, and touched him, and ***saith unto him, I will; be thou clean.*** *KJV*

Believe His promises just as you are! They are all ***"Yea and Amen in Christ!"*** Him who has called, chastened, promised and led you by the Holy Ghost to seek this Fountain opened for ***sin*** and ***uncleanness*** seals what He has done with a word from His lips. Just five little sentences may help you to grab hold of the Promise of the Father —

— ***What I give God takes.***
— ***What He takes He cleanses.***
— ***What He cleanses He fills.***
— ***What He fills He seals.***
— ***What He seals He uses.***

Let your FAITH — not your **understanding** — lead you up these easy steps; slowly, test each one as you take it. They will bear your weight; lean hard; walk firmly; and shout **"Excelsior"** as you rise – keep climbing, keep praising! So shall the work be done.

(excelsior adj. Latin.ever upward)

The way you receive this glorious blessing from God is in just the simple fashion and steps that I have placed before you. You can experience ***Promise Land living*** here and now, in this life. You do not have to stand on Jordan's stormy banks and cast a wistful eye — ***Beulah Land***_ is a gift of God in the work of ***"sanctification entire"***, and it is a present inheritance. You can experience it if you grasp the promises and believe, even as you believed to experience salvation. That wonderful land of promise is in Christ Jesus.

"Is Not This The Land Of Beulah?"
(Hymn/Anonymous Song of Experience_

Points To Ponder

1. What is a gift, is it earned, deserved ? Explain your concept of God's gift of John 3:16.________________

____

____

____

____

2. What is the purpose in God's chastening of the "child of God" ? ____

____

____

3. What is the Divine Nature of God ? ____________,

______________, __________, _________ .

4. What is the "central agent " in salvation, how is it accomplished ? __________________________________

____

5. What is the "central agent " in sanctification, how is it accomplished ? ________________________________

____

6. Explain the part each person in the eternal God-Head plays in the act of salvation, what is God's part, what is Jesus' part, what is the Holy Spirit's part ?

____

____

____

____

____

1. Explain the part of each person of the eternal God-Head plays in the act of sanctification, what is God's part, what is Jesus' part, what is the Holy Spirit's

part?

8. What role does the written "Word" play in both salvation and sanctification ?

Lesson Five

Holiness – It's Time

Heb 3:7

Wherefore as the Holy Ghost saith, To day if ye will hear his voice,

This is our fifth lesson of a seven part study, and perhaps the most important on understanding biblical **"Sanctification."** We have seen the ***necessity***, the ***nature*** and the ***way*** of God's sanctifying grace, and now we seek to know **WHEN** it can be ours. When can we enter the land of rest from the nature of Adam, and receive the abiding Comforter within our hearts?

To this question there is only one answer — **"NOW!"** Whether we enter it next week, next month, or next year, by the time that we get there it will be **NOW!** (The flow of time) So, why not to-day, why not this very hour?

The words of John Fletcher of Madeley, whom John Wesley considered the most saintly man he ever knew, expressed the imperative need to act now.

"Fight the good fight of faith, break through all temptations, dejections, wandering worldly thoughts, all unprofitable companions and the backwardness of an unbelieving heart, and a carnal mind. Struggle till you touch Jesus and feel healing, comforting virtue proceeding from Him, and when you know clearly the way to Him, repeat the touch till you find He lives in you by the powerful operation of His Holy Spirit."

Faith is a mighty living force wrought in us by the Holy Ghost, whereby we are enabled to lay hold upon Christ as our sanctification.

Therefore, in this fifth session, it will help us to consider the conditions under which a living, effective faith can operate to appropriate this full salvation.

— 1. Earnest Desire.......

Matt 5:6

Blessed are they which do **hunger and thirst** *after righteousness: for they shall be filled.*

Mark 11:24

Therefore I say unto you, What things soever **ye desire,** *when ye pray, believe that ye receive them, and ye shall have them. KJV*

Surely it is not error to say that in the hearts of many a great desire has been awakened for this blessed gift from the heavenly Father. The Lord Jesus, in speaking of the gift of the Holy Ghost in Luke 11:13, preludes that promise with a parable of a little hungry boy — not asking for game boys, or motorcycles, or "I"pods — but for bread and butter, the very necessities of life.

Luke 11:11-13

11 If a son shall ask bread of any of you that is a father, will he give him a stone? or if he ask a fish, will he for a fish give him a serpent?

12 Or if he shall ask an egg, will he offer him a scorpion?

13 If ye then, being evil, know how to give good gifts unto your children: how much more shall your heavenly Father give the Holy Spirit to them that ask him? KJV

Our children come home from school or from play and they are hungry and tired, and they do not fold their arms and say,

"Mom if it is your will to give us dinner tonight we would like to have it, but if not, then it will be all right, we will just do without."

Not hardly! They ask and make a noise until it is on the table and ready to eat. Are we like that spiritually for the gift of the Father? Are we hungry and thirsty for this heavenly gift? Is our soul fainting for this life of love, joy, peace and power? **Then faith can begin to operate here and this very moment if such is our deep desire.**

— 2. Conviction ....

Rom 12:1

*...that ye present your bodies a living sacrifice, holy, ...**which is your reasonable service**. KJV*

The second condition of an effective faith — is the recognition of the reasonableness of God's claims. I do not speak of the act of consecration itself, but rather of recognition of its reasonableness.

Do we believe that what God asks of us — which is a whole-hearted devotion to Himself, a true and loyal love to Him — is right, reasonable, and the best thing for us in all cases? To do His will is the safest, sweetest and surest thing on earth. Do you remember reading in the Word that Jesus said,

Matt 12:50

For whosoever shall do the will of my Father which is in heaven, the same is my brother, and sister, and mother. KJV

Jesus said it — therefore He meant it! What wonderful utterances to meditate upon! He that does God's will, the same is Christ's brother.

She that lives in the perfect will of our Father in heaven is the very mother or sister of the Saviour of the world. So to do that perfect will of God indeed is good and perfect and well-pleasing. This must be our objective. We must see that the sanctification we seek is from a heart that makes it possible to render a perfect consecration of **our entire being** to the Lord.

God must convict us of the unreasonableness of living for ourselves in any part of our life. Hunger and thirst — the deep desires of the soul — are followed or accompanied by a deep conviction that there is much within us, that does not bless His Holy Name and give an eager ***"YES"*** to all His reasonable demands for a ***wholly consecrated life.*** Let us close our eyes and stop our ears to anything and all things that would cause us to hold back from the reasonableness of God's holy claims.

— 3. Enlightenment ....

Ps 43:3
O send out thy light and thy truth: let them lead me; let them bring me unto thy holy hill, and to thy tabernacles.

Ps 119:105
Thy word is a lamp unto my feet, and a light unto my path. KJV

I am perfectly aware that we will not understand all of the blessedness of God grace, but still we appropriate it through the eyes of faith and as say ***"Amen."*** to all that it encompasses. My prayer must be for greater enlightenment and understanding, for then faith can operate with greater certainty. There are souls in different stages of development, needing different presentations of truth. I believe a little enlightenment will greatly increase the effective operation of faith.

Conversion or the ***New Birth*** deals largely with the conscience and the will of the unregenerate. The **"ego"** or **"self will"** is arrested and brought to the realization that His will is our only hope of salvation.

Sanctification on the other hand, deals with that which is:

Rom 7:17

17 Now then it is no more I that do it, **but sin that dwelleth in me** *.*

20 Now if I do that I would not, it is no more I that do it, but sin that dwelleth in me   KJV

There is a spiritual poison that lurks in our desires, affections, memory, mind and imagination that will rear its ugly head in unguarded moments. Just as the bacilli in the blood stream of a person with cancer — ***it is not part of them*** — it is an **abnormal intruder** in their system.

So it is with ***"the sin that dwelleth within."*** The **"I won't,"** the **"I can't,"** the **"I don't believe,"** is a spiritual virus that if not killed or chased out of the innermost being of the believer can develop into a poison that is fatal to the spiritual man.

We need a power from outside of ourselves to be the purging agent that will permeate the entire man, physical, mental, spiritual, and leave us a house swept and garnished and ***ready for the occupancy of the Divine Guest.***

Luke 11:25

...he findeth it swept and garnished .   KJV

Thank God His Word reveals to us that God has made such a provision for us. Listen to Paul's admonition:

1 Thess 4:3

For this is the will of God, even your sanctification,

1 Thess 5:23-24

23 And the very God of peace **sanctify you wholly***; and I pray God your* **whole spirit** *and* **soul** *and* **body** *be preserved blameless unto the coming of our Lord Jesus Christ.*

24 **Faithful is he that calleth you, who also will do it** *.*
KJV

May God make us earnestly see and believe for a perfect deliverance!

— 4. Repentance ....

Matt 3:8

Bring forth therefore fruits meet for repentance: KJV

Sometimes it would seem that some things are very confusing and hard to understand. Great truths are hidden from the casual gleaners eyes. More often than not they are not really ready for it. The truth is that before God can deal with the ***core of man's nature***, or they can by faith claim and trust Him for ***the purifying operation of the blood of Jesus***, there has to be a practical repentance.

There is, in short, real trouble in an un-surrendered will. God cannot deal with the ***inward man's struggle*** until we have dealt with the ***outward man in true repentance.*** I mention this rudimentary aspect because I am certain that there are numbers who are seeking an inward cleansing and filling — who in fact have not fully repented.

First things first — God requires a plain simple, straight forward practical repentance. That letter has to be written; that portion of money returned and made right; forgiveness has to be tendered to that one who wronged you; that hidden urge/temptation brought to light and dealt with. God cannot save over sin and certainly God will not sanctify with unresolved disobedience in the heart. **Restitution** is part of repentance that has long gone unresolved and unmentioned! To be sure wisdom must be used in this area and there are some things which cannot be resolved by restitution. In some instances there are "scrambled eggs" and no amount of effort, no matter how sincere can unscramble those situations. Those must be left with a wondrous God who has full knowledge and understanding of all that is involved. However, those things that we can set right, things which affect us but do not involve the wounding of others, we should make every effort to set right.

You will never receive further enlightenment until you have

fully accepted and embraced all the light you have already received. There is always a sense of rest following true repentance and obedience; but it is imperative that we press on to that perfection which the God of all grace has promised to do within us.

As I reflect upon my own life, how many those times of repentance loom large in my memory. Had not God given me grace to straighten out and make amends for acts, instances, and ignorance I would be on the outside looking in — ***instead of on the inside looking up!***

— 5. Humility ....

1 Peter 5:6

Humble yourselves therefore under the mighty hand of God, that he may exalt you in due time KJV

If I had to prioritize the simplest form of receiving heart purity from the hand of the risen exalted Christ I would say;

1. Humble yourselves under the mighty hand of God, *and*
2. Only believe! **Humility and faith is the way!**

Many make consecration or surrender the main element in securing the promised gift. Jesus did not say to his frightened, timid disciples behind closed doors when He appeared in their midst — ***"If you make a full and complete surrender I will give you the Holy Ghost."***

No! Indeed — for it is ALL grace — ALL a free gift — ALL of Him. The consecration ***FOLLOWS*** out of a grateful, thankful heart for what He had done and given!

I have encountered many as I have moved about the length and breadth of the country, and across the church who were in utter despair and weariness of spirit seeking the **"gift"** offered by the Father. What a joy it has been to proclaim to them the simple formula of ***"humility"*** and ***"faith"***.

John Wesley said that the ***"repentance of believers"*** is ***sine qua non*** (sign-***qway***-non) *[an indispensable or essential condition, element, or factor.]* Will you agree with me that the hardest people to get to fall on their faces, broken in spirit and pride, are ***"church"*** people? Listen to the ancient prophet:

2 Chron 7:14

If my people , which are called by my name, shall humble themselves, and pray, and seek my face, and turn from their wicked ways; then will I hear from heaven, and will forgive their sin, and will heal their land. KJV

Jealousy and envy are two wicked, ugly sisters. Envy has been called the green-eyed monster. Envy poisons contentment and destroys relationship and lives. It lurks furtively in the hidden hallways of the heart and slithers out unbidden. It feeds on feelings of insecurity, and it is one of the least confessed and most dangerous of sins. It can lead to slander and even murder *(killing another's reputation/influence).* ***Envy*** , along with her sister ***Jealousy*** , weeps when others rejoice and rejoices when other weep. It can be found in the home, the workplace, and around the church.

How do we confront such a subtle enemy?

— **First,** we honestly and humbly ask God to search out our hearts and see if envy - and/or - jealousy lurks there.

— **Second,** if God shows us their presence, we confront them and confess it.

— **Third,** we ask God to remove it and replace it with His own sweet Holy Spirit.

— **Finally,** we pray for those who are the object of our envy or jealousy.

Another danger area is pride. Pride is a subtle sin that walks hand-in-hand with envy and jealousy. Let me hasten to say that not all pride is sin. We should be proud of our children and grandchildren. We should take pride in being clean with the temple that God has given us to live in down here. We should be proud of our achievements and our compassion. We should be proud to be a child of God and a member of God's earthly family as well as His spiritual family. Nothing is wrong with this kind of pride. Even pride in our country is good and acceptable.

But when pride becomes swollen with ***SELF*** or when it clouds our better judgment and gives birth to the ***"top this"*** or ***"beat that"*** mind set, it turns into sin. Pride is the backdoor that Satan will use to bring down the house. Only ***the key of humility*** can keep that door locked and the way barred to the enemy of our souls.

1 Peter 2:9

But ye are a chosen generation, a royal priesthood, **an holy nation, a peculiar people***; that ye should shew forth the praises of him who hath called you out of darkness into his marvellous light:* KJV

— 6. Faith ....

Acts 15:9

And put no difference between us and them, ***purifying their hearts by faith.***

Gal 3:14

That the blessing of Abraham might come on the Gentiles through Jesus Christ; ***that we might receive the promise of the Spirit through faith.*** KJV

When shall we be sanctified? As soon as with deepest desire, convicted of our need, and of our impotence, enlightened as to the cause and seat of the lurking evil, truly repentant, and with genuine humility, we can ***"only believe"*** — then and there the blessing will be ours.

The Lord Jesus never said ***"only believe"*** to a Pharisee steeped in his own self-righteousness and formalism, nor to a Sadducee in his rationalism and so-called wisdom. He said it, and says it still, to the needy, penitent seeker, humbly bowed at His feet.

The **"HOW"** of faith ? We believe God through His promise and His Word; why try any other way? Rest in the Word — take hold of the definite explicit statements of the Lord. Throughout the Book there are ***"Thus saith the Lord."*** The apostles and the disciples were not the authors of these exceeding great and precious promises. They are the very words of God Himself. That is **HOW** to believe Him.

The hand of faith must have some explicit thing to grasp and to lay hold upon. It must — and Thank God it does have — The ***BLOOD*** of the Lamb, The ***CROSS*** of Calvary, The ***WOUNDS*** and ***STRIPES*** of Jesus.

Rev 7:14

These are they which came out of great tribulation, and have washed their robes, and made them white in the blood of the Lamb. KJV

If such was the case with those early conquerors through Christ, ***WHY not YOU?*** The ***"old man"*** was crucified with Christ, that the body of sin might be destroyed — then ***WHY not YOURS?*** *"Healed by His stripes..."* — then ***WHAT hinders YOU?***

The only reason that the Holy Guest of the Holy Ghost can bring an indwelling Christ into your heart is through the blood of the Lamb. The blood of Jesus is the price paid for this ***"divine blessing"*** That price is more than ample to satisfy the justice of God.

No tears, no consecrations, no vows, no fastings, or earnest endeavor, no struggles or good intentions will bring the Comforter to your soul. He responds to only one thing, the one and only thing — a bold, unswerving, unflinching faith in the sacrifice price paid at Calvary!

Faith must rest somewhere. When the devil rages and the storms of unbelief sweep over your soul, there is but one foundation that will stand the strain. ***Faith — Faith in God's Truth*** — my union with Him rests upon His death. ***He has cleansed me by His blood***, therefore He abides within. ***Here is faith's rock solid resting place***.

If the Comforter has not come into your life as yet, there is only one of two reasons — either you have not humbled yourself under the mighty hand of God, or ***you do not possess a believing faith***.

— 7. The Trial of Faith ....

James 1:3

Knowing this, that ***the trying of your faith*** *worketh patience. KJV*

This fact all who have been on the way for any length of time know from personal experience. Our walk is by faith, and faith alone! Look closely at 1 Peter 5:6 – 11:

1 Peter 5:6-11

6 **Humble yourselves therefore under the mighty hand of God**, that he may exalt you in due time:

7 **Casting all your care upon him**; *for he careth for you.*

8 Be sober, be vigilant; because your adversary **the devil,** *as a roaring lion, walketh about, seeking whom he may devour:*

9 Whom resist stedfast in the faith, *knowing that the same afflictions are accomplished in your brethren that are in the world.*

10 But the God of all grace, who hath called us unto his eternal glory by Christ Jesus, after that ye have suffered a while, make you perfect, stablish, strengthen, settle you.

11 To him be glory and dominion for ever and ever. Amen. KJV

Outlined there you find three condition on our part after which we read

"The God of all grace, **after that ye have suffered a little while** make you perfect, stablish, strengthen, settle you."

Plant a seed and it will stay beneath the cold dark clods of earth suffering a little while, and eventually dying — ***it is out of this death that there springs life!*** It is the very same with the seeds of faith!

Luke 17:6

If ye had **faith as a grain of mustard seed**, *ye might say unto this sycamine tree, Be thou plucked up by the root, and be thou planted in the sea; and it should obey you.* KJV

When you have definitely trusted and seem in utter darkness, say to yourself *"A little while....."* — then begin to praise by faith. Praise God and testify before men of what ***you believe that God has done in your soul.*** When the testing of your faith has done its work, the Holy Ghost ***will make real all that you have trusted Him for.***

When you have obeyed our Lord's words to the ruler of the synagogue ;

Mark 5:36

As soon as Jesus heard the word that was spoken, he saith unto the ruler of the synagogue, Be not afraid, only believe . KJV

Then the wings of faith will bear you up and in your own soul you will know that the very God of Peace Himself does sanctify you wholly and preserves you blameless, spirit, soul and body.

1 Thess 5:24

Faithful is he that calleth you, **who also will do it.** KJV

And you will praise Him throughout this life and as long as eternity rolls that He who has called you, has been faithful and **HAS DONE IT for you** — **even for you.** Praise His Holy Name

Points To Ponder

1. When can we possess this gift from God called "sanctification" ?

____

____

____

2. What are the conditions under which a living, victorious faith can operate effectively ? ______________,

______________, ______________, ______________ .

3. Explain "restitution" and its practical working in your life. Do you consider it necessary ? If not, why not ?

____

____

____

____

____

____

4. What is the "HOW" of faith?

____

____

____

____

5. What were the words of Jesus to the ruler of the synagogue ? How do they apply to your faith ?

____

____

Lesson Six

Holiness For The Whole Man

1 Thessalonians 5:

23 And the very God of peace sanctify you wholly; and I pray God your whole spirit and soul and body be preserved blameless unto the coming of our Lord Jesus Christ.

24 Faithful is he that calleth you, who also will do it. KJV

The Gospel of Jesus Christ is a holistic gospel for the whole man. Man has been called a triune entity according to the philosophy of the Apostle Paul and as evidenced in his writing to the Thessalonians which we use as our text for this lesson. Man is a trinity in other Scriptures as well — He is a trinity consisting of ***spirit*** — ***soul*** — and ***body***.

The ***spirit*** is the higher part, that which knows and is capable of God-consciousness, worship and communion ....receiving intuitively impression from the heavenly realm. It is the region of conscience, that which discerns between right and wrong, good and evil. Here it's voice is heard and it is the will — the king of man — that which chooses and shapes our destiny.

The ***spirit*** is the inner-man of the ***soul***, and possesses five senses; just as does the body. In one who is not a Christian these senses are unawakened. That the ***spirit*** and ***soul*** are not identical is proven by the Apostle in Hebrews 4:12 when speaking of the Word of God which:

...is quick, and powerful, and sharper than any twoedged sword, piercing even to **the dividing asunder of soul and spirit,** *and of the joints and marrow, and is a discerner of the thoughts and intents of the heart. KJV*

The spirit , soul, and body do not, of course, occupy separate space, but are like light, heat and air which fill the room simultaneously ! Man has been likened to a three-story building:

— **The basement, the lowest floor**, representing the ***body*** .

Multitudes live only in the basement — the base fleshly part of their natures. They are said to be **"carnal"** and their highest desire is to gratify the body with its attendant appetites and passions. This is the lowest plane of human living, it is the plane of the animal nature.

— **The first floor, the realm of the *soul* .** These folks live a step higher, dwelling in their emotions and affections. Art, music, literature, culture, and refinement appeal to them. This is humanism and as such is only a soulish natural life !

— **The top floor, the realm of the *spirit*.** God's thoughts and plan for His crowning creation, man, is that they live up in the spiritual realm where the spirit controls the entire man !

The ***spirit*** is not the emotional and intellectual part of man's being — this belongs to the ***soul*** ! The word **"spirit"** in the New Testament is *'pneuma'* ...... while that of the **"soul"** is the word *'psyche'* which means **"mind"**.

To say that spirit and soul are identical is to reduce Christianity to a mere intellectual state where our holy religion consists of holy tempers and sweet dispositions. There is a great deal of mental religion which consists of accepting Christ from a mental standpoint without any radical changing of the heart.

There is such a thing as having an emotional, soulish sensation and a so-called conversion without being regenerated in the higher, spiritual nature, where the conscience and will live and have their seat. The religion of some folks seems to consist principally by and through their emotions ! They can do questionable things and do not seem to suffer in their consciences. *(Sister Lola Morris tells of a man who stole a horse — but he could still speak in tongues, so the theft of the horse did not interfere with his religion.)*

Some are less than honest, hold on to fleshly habits and attitudes but let them get stirred in their emotions and they can make enough noise for a whole camp meeting. If we are not very careful, we might find ourselves shouting when we ought to be repenting if we just follow the dictates of emotions.

When the Bible speaks of the natural man receiving not the things of the ***Spirit of God***, neither being able to know them because they are spiritually discerned — the term PHYSICAL man is used. The natural *(physical)* man with all the gifts of culture and intellect included — may like Shakespeare, may like a composer like Mozart, or a painter like Raphael, an orator like Cicero, or a sculptor like Michelangelo and yet be only natural, earth-bound, time-bound and lost to the things and ways of God.

There can be no substitute for the Holy Ghost *!* All these things, though they are good, cannot be substituted for life in the **Spirit! What is meant by being sanctified in the threefold nature of man ?** We shall begin our explanation with the ***spirit*** for this is where the Apostle Paul begins in our text.

First — The Top Floor – A Sanctified Spirit

If you remember in the erection of the Tabernacle they began at the Holy of Holies, where the ***Shekinah*** glory dwelt! They then worked outward until the outer court was complete. When God makes a saint — **HE begins in the throne room of the spirit, where conscience reigns!**

****** ***To have a sanctified spirit means a purged conscience*** — which has been so *quickened–made alive* and sensitive to God and things divine that the least harsh or unkind word burns on the soul's sensibilities like a live coal ! It means a good conscience that makes us honest with ourselves, and will not allow us to convey to the public that which we do not possess within our own hearts.

It is a conscience so tender that it will not allow us to do small, mean, unkind, and underhanded tricks. There is no such thing as true piety without a live, quickened conscience ! Oh the stinging bite of a tender and sensitive conscience which is void of offense toward God and toward its fellow man ! Conscience, if I understand it correctly, has a fourfold function:

— 1. It is the still small voice of God in the soul, warning against wrong and wrongdoing.
— 2. It is a living witness and testifies against any and every wrong act or action.
— 3. It ascends the throne of judgment and proceeds to pronounce sentence against the guilty party.
— 4. It descends from the throne of judgment and lashes the soul with the scorpion's sting of an offended conscience before a holy God.

To have a Good Conscience means a restful, peaceful, purged conscience which is without accusation.

If our bodies are God's temples, than in these temples dwell the ***Holy Spirit*** — in the Holy of Holies – ***the heart*** — which is the ark of the covenant that holds the law of God within. Here, conscience, reigns like a heavenly queen approving the right and like the sting of the scorpion condemning the wrong ! Not only is the ***spirit*** the region of conscience, but it is that power that chooses, or to say it another way, **the will** .

*******A sanctified spirit* **means a conquered and totally subdued will !** If those who profess holiness were really subdued and broken in **will** — then God can get the workers which are needed! The **will** has two departments — *One* the power of choice and *Two* the power of perseverance to finish the course, whatever the cost !

The secret of Daniel and Joseph's strength of character was their **FIXED PURPOSE** to stay the course, so when the tests came, they continued as they had ***"Aforetime !"***

*******_**A sanctified spirit is a filled spirit**_ — one in which the image and likeness of Jesus is stamped, in which the spiritual senses are so clarified and quickened that *spiritual truths* become as real to that ***spirit***, as the physical world is to the natural senses.

******* ***A sanctified spirit is a clean spirit*** — the incoming of the Holy Ghost is first of all purifying. The order is first a purging, purifying, cleansing and then an empowering! There is a school of thinking which says that one can have power for service, but power for sinless living is disclaimed as impossible. There is no such thing as a ***spirit-filled life*** apart from a sanctification which is **entire** and **affects the total person !**

******* ***A sanctified spirit is a gentle spirit*** — one that is saved from harshness and roughness. A gentle spirit is a conquered and melted spirit. It has been bathed in a heavenly sea of tenderness and it can suffer injuries and receive all kinds of abuse and ill treatment without the boiling up of bitterness.

That is not to say that the sanctified person is beyond the possibility of experiencing negative emotions such as hurt feelings, impatience, worry, anxiety and such emotions. The sanctified may feel these emotions because one's emotional threshold may be affected by many things, such as illness, stress or pressure.

My purpose in mentioning these emotions and our responses to them is not to ***"whittle out"*** a loophole to let one crawl through, settle down and enjoy and indulge such emotions. Rather, my purpose is to help the sanctified avoid ***SELF-condemnation*** for normal, natural human conduct.

Remember, one has not sinned as long as his motives are pure and there is no rebellion. God's saints are a gentle people who are not in rebellion against God or any of His children. While we may have our times of lows and highs, we will never lash out to wound or hurt and deal harshly with those about us. Through tenderness of the conscience we are cognizant of the feelings of others and always endeavor to gently deal with them on all levels.

*******A sanctified spirit is a humble spirit*** — A holiness that does not produce humility is a sham and a spurious sort.

There is nothing more beautiful in the Christian experience than a real Christ-like spirit where all the self-life and religious human strut has been burned out. This kind of spirit does not have to be the **"bell sheep"** to be kept in good humor. It expects nothing and wonders at nothing that is done and is at perfect rest when nobody praises it. This is the kind of spirit that opens the gate of Heaven without touching it!

This is the spirit that wears out the patience of persecutors and softens the hearts of stone, that in the long run converts enemies into friends, that touches the hearts of sinners, and that wins its way through a thousand obstacles. It outwits the genius of the devil and makes the soul that has it as precious to God as the ***Apple of His Eye !*** How we, the church, need to pray that God would help His people to *attain* and *maintain* a **"sanctified spirit"** !

Now we move to the first floor and the subject of:

Second — A Sanctified Soul

The ***soul*** is the seat of the affections, understanding, emotions and tastes/appetites. We are told by the best scholars that the word ***"soul"*** translated in the Old Testament *"nephesh"* (*neh'*-fesh) is the exact equivalent of the New Testament word in the Greek of *"psyche"* (*psoo*-khay).

The ***soul***, with its emotions, sensibilities and affections is a little world within itself. It is like the ocean, with its storms and calms. Men have sailed its bosom, dived into it depths, walked up and down its shores, prospected for its treasures, studied it mystery and still there are depths which are hidden and unknown. **So It Is With The Human Soul** !

We notice from out text that the blessing of sanctification is related to our threefold nature — to the ***spirit*** and to the ***soul*** and to the ***body***. Considering our affections, we find that while they are not sinful within themselves, there are in a fallen state and often prove an easy channel for sin to rear its ugly head.

Many times we see a beautiful vine clinging to a rotten tree just ready to fall, or to some tottering old wall just at the verge of crumbling. I say that to say this: Have we not all seen a beautiful life ruined by allowing its affections to cling to some human idol or to some forbidden object?

The nature of the vine is to reach upward, to climb higher, so the ***Holy Ghost***, in conversion gently unwinds our affections from the low and the earthly things and begins to entwine them around things above. It is in sanctification that we are purified, refined, enlarged and sweetened until even our love for friends is deeper and purer and holier.

The Bible speaks of an inordinate affection which we are to mortify and put to death, along with uncleanness and fleshly lusts.

Galatians 5:

24 And they that are Christ's have crucified the flesh with the affections and lusts.

25 If we live in the Spirit, let us also walk in the Spirit. KJV

There is a kind of earthly, sensual love which God says must be crucified if we live in the ***Spirit.*** Some of the darkest crimes of the ages began in the channel of unsanctified affections.

Samson could strangle young lions, pick up ponderous brazen gates, slay whole armies ... but he went down with a crash through unsanctified affections. There are thousands of shorn Samsons today who have had their spiritual locks clipped and have been robbed of their power by following inordinate affections. Sin binds, sin grinds, and sin blinds ! ***NO ONE IS SAFE WITH AN UNSANCTIFIED NATURE !***

1 Thessalonians 5:23

And the very God of peace sanctify you **wholly**; *and I pray God your whole* ***spirit*** *and* **soul** *and* ***body*** *be preserved blameless unto the coming of our Lord Jesus Christ.* *KJV*

The ***soul*** embraces the understanding which has several departments, involving thought, reason, judgment, the store house of memory and the faculty of the imagination or image room. *(Chambers of his imagery.)*

Ezekiel 8:12

Then said he unto me, Son of man, hast thou seen what the ancients of the house of Israel **do in the dark, every man in the chambers of his imagery?** *for they say, The Lord seeth us not; the Lord hath forsaken the earth.* *KJV*

When we stop to think how our future life is molded by our thoughts, and how the mind controls the body, and how the imagination, like an artist with brush in hand, is constantly painting pictures — how absolutely essential it is to have all the powers and faculties brought under the control and subjection to the ***Holy Ghost*** !

It is a psychological fact that to follow in any one line of thinking produces narrow, neural paths or brain channels making it easy to continue in that channel and thus form a fixed thought habit. It is dangerous to allow this process to go unchecked and unrestrained for it will drive wedges of division and ill-will where there is none, nor ever been reason for such feelings.

It is easy to see the importance of entertaining pure thoughts and rejecting impure ones. Evil thoughts are like seeds blown by the wind, if allowed to remain, and if kept warm by consent, they **WILL** produce a harvest of sin. Here is some old farm boy, mountain logic: ***Chilled eggs never hatch !*** We can **CHILL** impure suggestions and thoughts by refusing to entertain them!

In considering the storehouse of memory it is the mission of the ***Comforter*** to bring all things to our remembrance concerning spiritual matters of the ***soul.*** It is wonderful how the mind, under the enlightenment of the ***Holy Ghost*** becomes alive, grasping the spiritual truth of God with vigor and clarity that would be impossible without this divine illumination.

It is like depositing money into a savings account with a bank — memory will bring them back to the consciousness when the need for them arrives. One of the blessed consolations of old age is that we can recall a life spent well in the service of our God and the quest for lost souls through a ***sanctified memory.***

Another department of the mind is ***the imagination or the image-room,*** where all kinds of pictures are painted and hung upon the walls of the ***soul*** ! The imagination is that power that can create a world of its own fancy. It can cross oceans or reach the most distant star in the galaxy.

The devil can take advantage of this faculty and use it to the destruction of the individual. The imagination has been likened to an island which is visited by its owner on a regular basis. At this island of imagination the young girl comes and spends hours, but on her return she would not for the world permit her mother to know where she has been.

There comes a married man who also spends hours under those beautiful shade trees while his faithful wife all the while is unconscious of what he has done and is doing in this dangerous and deadly place. *(Remember the TV show "Fantasy Island"?)*

How true it is that without even leaving the room, trips may be taken where the vilest of earth is mingled and the dearest of ties is violated. Such is the world of the internet and where people go when there — it has become the physical manifestation of the mind's image-room or imagination !

Oh how we need to crush the head of the serpent of **UN-holy imagination.** This is what the Apostle meant by:

2 Corinthians 10:5

Casting down imaginations, *and every high thing that exalteth itself against the knowledge of God, and bringing into captivity every thought to the obedience of Christ;* KJV

The ***Holy Spirit*** does not destroy this wonderful faculty of imagination in sanctifying us — He only purifies it until thought pictures can be painted of Jesus, of heaven, of the return of our Lord, of the holiness of God and of godly things to replace the hangings upon the walls of the ***soul.***

Next comes the emotions of the ***soul*** — Psychologists have classified these into 42 separate emotions distinct for one another.

We are only going to consider a couple:

— There are the **pure** and the **impure.**
— There are the **holy** and the **unholy.**

All pure emotions, such as joy, peace, kindness, gentleness, love, are constructive and are real health-builders. For example *LOVE* — it can transform any condition of life and make the heart that once was a nest of vipers blossom like the flower must have in God's Eden. Love drives out all hatred, malice, envy, strife, and bitterness from the soul and at the same time starts emotions working until every part of the mental and physical being is affected ! Love puts a gentle tone in the voice and a tender look in the eye that changes the expression of the whole face.

There is nothing more beautiful than pure, radiant *JOY.* Joy is the best stimulant and tonic that has been found for soul and body. It drives the blues away and puts fears to flight. The Bible tells us that joy and laughter is as medicine to the soul !

PEACE quiets the nerves and takes the tiredness and careworn look from the face, and leaves in its place the soft, love-light from the hills of glory imprinted upon the countenance.

KINDNESS has a reaction on the heart. It is impossible to do a kind act without being repaid in a sweetness that is beyond expression. While this is true, it is also true that hatred, malice, jealousy and envy have a killing effect on all the faculties of ***soul*** and ***body***.

ANGER is like a raging inferno! It elevates the heart rate, weakens the ***body*** worse than a fever. It poisons the blood and undermines the general health and well-being of the angered one.

Then there is *MALICE* — which is anger cooled off ! It dries up all the finer sensibilities of the soul and puts a hardness upon the heart and the face of the one who bears malice. *(Old Mose and salvation gland.)* The great blessing of *sanctification entire* is that it is God's remedy for every emotion of the ***soul*** , every need of the ***body*** and every quest of the ***spirit*** !

Finally, ***the soul possesses the faculty of TASTE.*** Just as the taste of the mouth decides the kind of food that we take into our bodies, so the inner taste of the soul decides the character of spiritual food that is to be taken into the moral and spiritual life.

Unless our *musical taste* is sanctified and dedicated to God it will prove a snare instead of a blessing. There is our *viewing taste* which must be sanctified as to what we watch and consume through the eye-gate. There is the *reading taste* that must be sanctified or we will take into our minds that which is base and debilitating rather than enlightening.

A ***sanctified taste*** has no secret longing for the tawdry things of life, for worldly entertainment and amusement, for worldly adornment, for low grade literature, and the party spirit of this world. The ***sanctified heart*** sings:

> *"There's no thirsting for life's pleasures nor adorning rich and gay,*
> *For I've found a greater treasure, one that*
> *fadeth not away......!"*

Last of all, we now come to the **BASEMENT** of man for consideration of ***A Sanctified Body.*** There are enough mysteries connected with the human body to convince the most incredulous mind of the existence of an omnipotent God. It is no wonder that the "Sweet Singer of Israel" cries out:

4 What is man, that thou art mindful of him? and the son of man, that thou visitest him?
5 For thou hast made him a little lower than the angels, Psalms 8:4-5 KJV

There is an infinite, impassable gulf between the most poorly developed human body and the highest of the brute beast of the forest or field. Man has been called God's Masterpiece. We get some conception of what he is when we see how God created him with faculties that are capable of God-consciousness, and cravings that are eternal. Nobody or nothing else has this capacity, it is innate in man alone !

It was believed and taught in the **dark ages** that the body was vile, the seat of sin and the only way to rid it of sin was to punish it. This gave rise to self flagellation. Yet after such treatment sin still remained. Sin is not located in the flesh, bone, sinew, blood, nor nerve system. You might cut the body to ribbons, but still sin will not be destroyed.

Others of that era retired to monasteries and convents to find deliverance from sin — but some of the most wicked spirits to be found were in the monk in his cell. Still others tried to starve sin out of the body by fasting and praying. Some fasted so long that they became skeletons and still the **"old man"** remained. Sin does not live in flesh and blood nor in bread and meat.

Thank God for the blessedness of genuine "holiness" that can be in the world, yet not of the world !

The Adam nature cannot be "suppressed" as many teach, and it cannot be ignored so that it will go away as the Keswick be teaching that it is made ***"null and void"***. Neither can it be educated and trained out by polishing and improving. The Apostle calls the carnal mind an outlaw and he says it is not subject to the law of God. You may dress up old Adam, and you may polish him and train him, but you have not changed his nature — he is still a son of Adam, not a Son of God !

Romans 8:7

Because the carnal mind is enmity against God: for it is not subject to the law of God, neither indeed can be. KJV

You will have to go deeper than education, culture and polished manners to get rid of the carnal mind. ***God's more excellent way is to make the body a temple for the Holy Ghost to occupy !***

The Greek word "soma" or body has a twofold meaning with the **outer part** and the **inner part** of the body conveying different meanings. The meaning of the **outer division** is the organized physical body, with its attendant flesh, bones and blood — the **inner part** is designed as the seat of the passions, appetites and desires. **This Is The Part With Which The Holy Ghost Deals !**

What is a ***sanctified body*** ? It is a body that is saved and cleansed from sin. God's Plan is for the **spiritual nature** to control the **physical nature** and the more one lives in the realm of the ***Spirit***, the less trouble will be had with the body in the sin arena.

A ***sanctified body*** is a dedicated body with ALL its members and faculties relinquished to the ***Holy Ghost's*** control and the reins freely placed in God's hands.

— The **TONGUE** while a little member, has the power to wreak deadly evil. A sanctified tongue is one that is saved not only from the falsehoods of every form, but from gossip, slander, and idle talk.

Leviticus 19:16

Thou shalt not go up and down as a talebearer among thy people: KJV

There is nothing more hurtful than the slanderous tongue with its blistering touch. Homes have been broken and families torn asunder because of this instrument untamed. An unbridled tongue is a sure sign of an unsanctified heart ! *Be sure my friend YOUR tongue is sanctified and surrendered to the control of the Holy Ghost.*

— A ***sanctified body*** means **cleansed eyes** that refuse to gaze upon an impure object. If you recall the story of the fall, it stemmed from that which entered through the channel of the eyes !

Genesis 3:6

And when **the woman saw** *that the tree was good for food, and that it was pleasant to the eyes, and a tree to be desired to make one wise, she took of the fruit thereof, and did eat, and gave also unto her husband with her; and he did eat.*

The eye was the downfall of David, the great king, and of Lot's dilemma when he ***"looked toward Sodom....".*** All that followed began by an improper look. No man can keep sanctified and gaze at the impure, the unholy objects of this sensual age. Folks we must make sure that we draw the blinds from this world filled with evil at every hand.

— A ***sanctified body*** is one **WHOSE EARS ARE DEDICATED TO GOD.** They have lost all desire for gossip, for talebearing and tidings of evil. A person who will lend their ears to listen to a slanderous report and feel inwardly tickled, is just as evil as the person who is doing the slander. ***Sanctified ears*** are dedicated to hear the *"still small voice of God."*

— A ***sanctified body*** is one that **DRESSES FOR THE GLORY OF THE LORD.** Such will robe/clothe itself in modest apparel as becomes

saints and not following the herd instinct of worldly fad and fashion. The standards have been so lowered in our present culture until modesty is almost a thing of the past.

Thank God for a **HOLINESS** that touches the threefold nature of man, causing him to live where the ***Shekinah glory*** of God can abide. From that fire inside the ***sanctified heart*** the light shines forth through every part and faculty of ***spirit,*** of ***soul***, and of ***body***. In a **sanctification which is entire !** The ***"old man"*** has been crucified and the ***"new man"*** in Christ is enthroned within. ***Praise the Lord !***

Points To Ponder

1. Man is a _____________, consisting of _____________, _____________. and ___________ .

2. How is man compared to a three story building ?

____
____
____
____
____

3. To have a sanctified spirit means to have a purged ___________________, a ___________ and _________ spirit, a ________ spirit , a __________ spirit, a ___________ spirit, and a ____________ spirit.

4. The soul of man is the seat of ___________, ___________, ___________, and ___________, ___________ .

5. What are we to do with inordinate affections according to Galatians 5:24, 25 ?

____
____

6. According to the biblical account of Sampson, sin _________, sin __________, and sin __________.

7. What was Ezekiel *(in Ezekiel 8:12)* talking about when he spoke of the "chambers of imagery "?____
____
____
____

8. What is a sanctified body ?

____

____

____

____

9. In a sanctified body name at least three parts of the body that are under the complete control of the Holy Spirit. The _____________, the ____________, and the _____________.

10 In your own words give a definition of the “old man” and the “new man” ____

____

____

____

____

____

Chapter Seven

Holiness (*Sanctification*)

A Process, A Crisis, Or Both

1Thes 4:

1 Furthermore then we beseech you, brethren, and exhort you by the Lord Jesus, that as ye have received of us how ye ought to walk and to please God, so ye would abound more and more.

2 For ye know what commandments we gave you by the Lord Jesus.

3 For this is the will of God, even your sanctification, that ye should abstain from fornication:

4 That every one of you should know how to possess his vessel in sanctification and honour; (KJV)

Does the experience of sanctification result from growth and self-discipline, or is it an act of God's grace completed in a moment of time?

This is a question that has complicated and confused the minds and hearts of countless saints of God. There are strong and articulate proponents on both sides of this gripping issue.

It is not my intent to add fuel to the fires of controversy. My purpose and intent is to present as clearly, precisely, and as intelligently as I can what the ***Word of God*** says on this crucial issue that confronts every **"Born Again"** believer.

Those who advocate a ***progressive work*** advance the idea that the sin nature may be progressively brought under control, mortified daily by careful attention to the means of grace, and that the believer is being progressively sanctified by gaining greater and greater victory over sin in his life, and more and more control over the impulses of sin in his heart.

To the other side of the equation stands the holiness camp who understand **"Sanctification Entire "** as an instantaneous act wrought by the Holy Ghost in a moment of time. It is as perfect and complete in its kind as the work of regeneration, as justification is perfect and complete in its kind. This does not mean that there is no growth in grace both before and after sanctification. What it does mean is that sanctification, ***as an act of God, <u>is instantaneous,</u>*** and is not produced by growth or self-discipline or the progressive control of the carnal nature.

1. Sanctification by Growth

Before we get to ***"Thus saith the Lord....."*** let me give a brief consideration to the growth, or progressive theory.

First: It is difficult to see in this anything more than a rejection of the blood in favor of sanctification *by human striving and works.* Pious words are uttered about the help of the Holy Spirit while the possibility of His instantaneous work is denied. It is possible to give lip service to the Spirits's ministry and at the same time flatly to contradict His sanctifying lordship!

Second: ***Death*** is expected to complete what grace and the cross of Christ could not! Lurking back of these speculations is the ghost of the ancient ***Gnostic heresy***, which is that the physical body is in some sense the seat and source of sin.

Otherwise, there is no logical reason for this persistent doubt that the redeemed soul may be free from sin here and now!

Third: The fact is that the Bible never intimates anywhere that either ***growth*** or ***death*** have the least thing to do with the soul's sanctification! Instead....the ***Word of God***, the ***Blood of Christ***, the ***Holy Spirit***, and ***faith*** are the factors indicated as being concerned with sanctification.

Growth is referred to as being **IN** grace, never **INTO** grace! Growth always relates to increase in ***" quantity "***, never to change in ***" quality "***

To suppose that ***physical death*** makes any change in the moral quality of the human's soul is to go in direct opposition to the clear declarations of the ***Word of God!***

2. Sanctification A Crisis Experience

Turning now to the testimony of the ***Word*** we find it is a ***crisis experience*** and not an endless process that starts with salvation and ends with death. Let me qualify what I am saying when I speak of sanctification as " **entire** ".

1 Thess 5:23-24

23 And the very God of peace ***sanctify you wholly;*** *and I pray God your* **whole spirit** *and* **soul** *and* **body** *be preserved blameless unto the coming of our Lord Jesus Christ.*

24 **Faithful is he that calleth you, who also will do it.**
KJV

Did you pick up on **WHO** does this work? It is not our progressive effort that brings about this experience — **it is God who does this work!** And **HE** does it to the **WHOLE** man, the **ENTIRE** being!

In the Word we find three classes of evidence that the act of ***sanctification*** is **entire** , in fact, and is ***instantaneous*** and not a gradual or progressive act.

— **1. There is the analogy to the New Birth and justification.**

— **2. There is the testimony of the terms used to describe the work.**

— **3. There is the logic of example found in**

the Bible.

Let's look briefly at each of them:

First— The Analogy with the New Birth. Think with me if you will of the analogy found in the Bible between justification or the New Birth **(The First work of the Spirit.)** and sanctification or heart purity **(The Second work of the Spirit)**. There are great points of similarity between these two works of divine grace.

—Both justification and sanctification are products of divine love:

John 3:16

For God so loved the world, that he gave his only begotten Son, that whosoever believeth in him should not perish, but have everlasting life. (KJV)

Eph 5:25-27

25 Husbands, love your wives, even as Christ also loved the church, and gave himself for it;

26 That he might sanctify and cleanse it with the washing of water by the word,

27 That he might present it to himself a glorious church, not having spot, or wrinkle, or any such thing; but that it should be holy and without blemish. (KJV)

—Both justification and sanctification are manifestations of God's good, acceptable, and perfect will:

1 Tim 2:3-4

3 For this is good and acceptable in the sight of God our Saviour;

4 Who will have all men to be saved, and to come unto the knowledge of the truth. (KJV)

Heb 10:10

By the which will **[that is, the will of God as accomplished by Christ in His atoning death]** *we are* *sanctified through the offering of the body of Jesus Christ once for all. (KJV)*

—Both justification and sanctification are accomplished through the wonderful light of God's Word:

1 Pet 1:23

Being born again, not of corruptible seed, but of incorruptible, by the word of God, which liveth and abideth for ever. (KJV)

John 17:17

Sanctify them through thy truth: thy word is truth. (KJV)

—Both justification and sanctification are wrought in the heart by the effective agency of the Holy Spirit of God:

Titus 3:3

For we ourselves also were sometimes foolish, disobedient, deceived, serving divers lusts and pleasures, living in malice and envy, hateful, and hating one another. (KJV)

II Th 2:13

But we are bound to give thanks alway to God for you, brethren beloved of the Lord, because God hath from the beginning chosen you to salvation through sanctification of the Spirit and belief of the truth: (KJV)

—Both justification and sanctification are purchased at the cost of Christ's shed blood on Calvary's cross:

Rom 5:9

Much more then, being now justified by his blood, we shall be saved from wrath through him. (KJV)

Heb 13:12

Wherefore Jesus also, that he might sanctify the people

with his own blood, suffered without the gate. (KJV)

—Both justification and sanctification are brought to the individual believer's heart in response to faith:

Rom 5:1

Therefore being justified by faith, we have peace with God through our Lord Jesus Christ: (KJV)

Acts 26:18

To open their eyes, and to turn them from darkness to light, and from the power of Satan unto God, that they may receive forgiveness of sins, and inheritance among them which are sanctified by faith that is in me. (KJV)

Virtually all Bible-believing Christians acknowledge that the New Birth *(justification)* is not a gradual process, but is an instantaneous act. It is an act of God which takes place at a given point in a believer's life.

It happens the very instant that they accept God's Son as their Saviour by faith!

If both ***justification*** and ***sanctification*** are products of the same divine love, the same will of God, the same Holy Word, the same blessed Holy Spirit, the same redeeming blood, the same human condition — **which is faith — is there any valid reason for supposing that one is instantaneous while the other is gradual and by a growth process ?**

If ***justification*** is instantaneous, there is certainly no reason why ***sanctification***, wrought by the same agency, the Holy Spirit, should not be equally the act of a moment.

As a matter of fact, every argument which proves the instantaneity of regeneration is just as valid when applied to sanctification! If the evidence for the immediacy of sanctification is rejected, there is no logical ground on which to base proof for the immediacy of justification!

Rom 5:1-2

1 Therefore being justified by faith, we have peace with God through our Lord Jesus Christ:

2 By whom also we have access by faith into this grace wherein we stand, and rejoice in hope of the glory of God. KJV

Second: The Testimony of the Terms

We must look at the terms used to describe this second work in the Christian heart. Without exception, the root action is such as to imply ***that which occurs at a particular point in time.***

The verb ***"to sanctify"*** is defined in its twofold meaning as ***"to set apart"*** and ***"to make holy."*** There may, it is true, be a gradual setting apart, a gradual making holy.....**but the action described is much more naturally thought of as momentary and immediate.**

Since ***"to sanctify"*** in its strictly New testament sense is always spoken of as a **divine act,** the burden of proof ought naturally to rest upon those who allege sanctification to be gradual.

For example — you will notice, this experience is spoken of as a baptism!

Acts 1:5

For John truly baptized with water; but ye shall be baptized with the Holy Ghost not many days hence. (KJV)

"Baptism" is not a term which is drawn out over a long period of time, and perhaps never completed until death. Gradual baptism is an absurdity— whether it be a baptism with water, or the baptism with the Holy Spirit.

Sanctification spoken of as a crucifixion or death.

Rom 6:6

Knowing this, that our old man is crucified with him, that the body of sin might be destroyed, that henceforth we should not serve sin. (KJV)

Gal 2:20

I am crucified with Christ: nevertheless I live; yet not I, but Christ liveth in me: and the life which I now live in the flesh I live by the faith of the Son of God, who loved me, and gave himself for me. (KJV)

Col 3:5

Mortify **[treat as dead]** *therefore your members which are upon the earth; fornication, uncleanness, inordinate affection, evil concupiscence, and covetousness, which is idolatry: (KJV)*

I will grant you that a person may be long in dying.....however, ***death*** always occurs in a moment! Life may wane over a period of time, but it departs the body in an instant! Gradual death is a figure of speech for a fatal or terminal illness.....death itself is always instant- aneous!

Sanctification involves cleansing, purifying.

The Bible is replete with the uses of the verbs **"cleanse"** — **"purify."**

Acts 15:8-9

8 And God, which knoweth the hearts, bare them witness, giving them the Holy Ghost, even as he did unto us;

9 And put no difference between us and them, **purifying their hearts by faith**. *KJV*

Eph 5:25-27

25 Husbands, love your wives, even as Christ also loved the church, and gave himself for it;

26 ***That he might sanctify and cleanse it*** *with the washing of water by the word,*
27 That he might present it to himself a glorious church, not having spot, or wrinkle, or any such thing; but that it should be holy and without blemish. (KJV)

Cleansing and purification may be continuous processes, but the natural meaning of these words indicate that **there is always an initial moment when the cleansing and purification begins.**

To make it gradual is to read into it something which the words themselves certainly do not imply!

Sanctification is described as a "GIFT" to be "RECEIVED".

Luke 11:13
If ye then, being evil, know how to give good gifts unto your children: how much more shall your heavenly Father give the Holy Spirit to them that ask him? (KJV)

Gal 3:14
That the blessing of Abraham might come on the Gentiles through Jesus Christ; that we might receive the promise of the Spirit through faith. (KJV)

Is it not a fact that a gift is something which passes into the possession of the receiver from the giver at some given moment? Who ever heard of someone gradually giving another a gift?

Sanctification is variously described as **"putting off"** the old man and **"putting on"** the new.

Eph 4:20-24
20 But ye have not so learned Christ;
21 If so be that ye have heard him, and have been taught by him, as the truth is in Jesus:
22 That ye put off concerning the former conversation

the old man, which is corrupt according to the deceitful lusts;
23 And be renewed in the spirit of your mind;
24 And that ye put on the new man, which after God is created in righteousness and true holiness. (KJV)

"To set apart," "to make holy," "to baptize," "to crucify," "to put to death," "to give," "to receive," "to put off," "to put on," "to destroy,""to be filled," "to be sealed" these are all verbs describing actions which take place most naturally at a definite time and place and not by degrees or a gradual process.

They all testify to the fact that sanctification is a crisis experience subsequent to salvation and not a long-drawn-out and never-completed process of growth!

3. The Logic of Example....

This is the final line of evidence for the instantaneity of entire sanctification, based upon scriptural examples.

The experience of Isaiah recorded in Isaiah 6 may be regarded as a type of the believer's experience of entire sanctification. Isaiah had been a prophet of God during part of the reign of King Uzziah, as he tells us in chapter one. But it was in the year the king died that God's prophet experienced his remarkable cleansing.

In the Temple worshiping, Isaiah saw the Lord high and lifted up, and heard the seraphs' song, ***"Holy, holy, holy, is the Lord of hosts"***. That praise of God's holiness found no echo in the prophet's heart, and he who had just called ***"woe's"*** on the people now cried out for himself....:

Isa 6:5
*Then said I, **Woe is me!** for I am undone; because I am a man of unclean lips, and I dwell in the midst of a people of unclean lips: ...(KJV)*

The divine response was not long in coming. And angel flew

with golden tongs and a live coal from the altar, touched his lips, and said,

Isa 6:6-7

6 Then flew one of the seraphims unto me, having a live coal in his hand, which he had taken with the tongs from off the altar:

7 And he laid it upon my mouth, and said, ***Lo, this hath touched thy lips; and thine iniquity is taken away, and thy sin purged.*** *(KJV)*

This all took place in less time than it takes to describe. It was not by growth or spiritual development that Isaiah's iniquity was taken away and his sin purged. It was by a divine act at a given time.

— **A second biblical example** is found in the Book of Acts. It records events surrounding the young church in Samaria. Phillip had ventured into Samaria after the martyrdom of Stephen. His preaching was received warmly and embraced for the citizens of that country. The people believed and were baptized in large numbers. Acts records that there was great joy in the city;

Acts 8:6-8

6 And the people with one accord gave heed unto those things which Philip spake, hearing and seeing the miracles which he did.

7 For unclean spirits, crying with loud voice, came out of many that were possessed with them: and many taken with palsies, and that were lame, were healed.

8 **And there was great joy in that city.** *(KJV)*

News of this revival and the success of the ministry of the Word soon reached the apostles in Jerusalem. They sent Peter and John to investigate. When they came, we read that they prayed for these young converts;

Acts 8:15-17

15 Who, when they were come down, prayed for them, **that they might receive the Holy Ghost:**
16 (For as yet he was fallen upon none of them: only they were baptized in the name of the Lord Jesus.)
17 Then laid they their hands on them, **and they received the Holy Ghost!**

The Samaritans believed and were baptized under the ministry of the Holy Ghost and Phillip, and they were afterwards filled with the Holy Ghost when Peter and John came down from Jerusalem, and it was done at a given instant in time.....not a progressive process.

— ***A third example*** concerns the devout Roman centurion Cornelius and members of his household. Cornelius is described in no uncertain terms by God's inspired penman:

Acts 10:2
A devout man, and one that feared God with all his house, which gave much alms to the people, and prayed to God alway. (KJV)

His prayers reached God's throne and gained audience before the eternal God:

Acts 10:4
... And he said unto him, **Thy prayers and thine alms are come up for a memorial before God.** *(KJV)*

Peter arrives on the scene and makes this quick assessment:

Acts 10:34-35
34 Then Peter opened his mouth, and said, Of a truth I perceive that God is no respecter of persons:
35 But in every nation he that feareth him, and worketh righteousness, is accepted with him. (KJV)

As Peter continues to speak, **suddenly the Holy Ghost fell** on those who listened. This was not a gradual happening....it was instantaneous! Peter regarded the events at Cornelius' home as ***parallel with and identical*** to the events at Pentecost. This is clearly seen in his report to the council at Jerusalem:

Acts 15:8-9
8 And God, which knoweth the hearts, bare them witness, giving them the Holy Ghost, even as he did unto us;
9 And put no difference between us and them, purifying their hearts by faith. KJV

— ***A fourth instance given in the Acts*** is described in Acts 18:25 — Acts 19:7. It concerns the disciples at Ephesus. At the close of the Apostle Paul's long ministry in Corinth, he, in company with Aquila and Priscilla crossed the Aegean Sea to the mainland of Asia and to the city of Ephesus. Paul spent only a short time there preaching in the synagogue and, leaving Aquila and Priscilla there, he went on toward Antioch.

While Paul was gone, and man named Apollos came to Ephesus. Apollos was eloquent, mighty in the scriptures, spoke diligently the things of the Lord, although, as far as baptism was concerned, he knew only the baptism of John. Recognizing the potential greatness of Apollos' ministry, Aquila and Priscilla took him and, as we read, taught him the way of God more perfectly.

Acts 18:24-26
24 And a certain Jew named Apollos, born at Alexandria, an eloquent man, and mighty in the scriptures, came to Ephesus.
25 This man was instructed in the way of the Lord; and being fervent in the spirit, he spake and taught diligently the things of the Lord, knowing only the baptism of John.
26 And he began to speak boldly in the synagogue: whom when Aquila and Priscilla had heard, they took him unto them, and expounded unto him the way of God more perfectly. (KJV)

Shortly after Apollos left his new-found friends, Aquila and Priscilla to go to Corinth, Paul came back to Ephesus. Upon arrival there Paul found in Ephesus a nucleus of twelve disciples. Upon examining them, he learned that they had not received the Holy Ghost, at least in the measure of Pentecost. But after Paul had baptized them in the name of Christ, he prayed, laid hands upon them, and they were filled with the Holy Ghost.

The misunderstanding which surrounds this incident has to do with the spiritual status of the Ephesian disciples. Because they had no knowledge of the Holy Spirit, and because they had received only the baptism of John, some have contended that they were not saved men.

That these twelve men were genuine children of God, and that this was for them a subsequent experience of the in-filling of the Holy Ghost is clearly set forth in the context.

— **First**, the men were described as ***disciples*** (Acts 19:1).

Acts 11:26
26 ...And the disciples were called Christians first in Antioch. (KJV)

There is no instance of the use of the term ***"disciple"*** in the Acts for any other than true believers in Christ! These men were ***"disciples"***! Notice also that Paul did not challenge the fact of their faith.

Acts 19:2
*2 He said unto them, Have ye received the Holy Ghost **since ye believed?** ...... (KJV)*

The fact that they were ignorant of the receiving of the Holy Ghost does not mean that they were unconverted. It just high-lights the fact that they were uninformed that the Holy Ghost was the third person of the eternal God-head.

Nor does the fact that these men had only received the baptism of John prove that they were unconverted in the full Christian sense of the word. In fact, the baptism of John is spoken of as a ***"baptism of repentance unto the remission of sins."***

Mark 1:4

John did baptize in the wilderness, and preach the baptism of repentance for the remission of sins. (KJV)

Apollos, instructed in the way of the Lord, fervent in the Spirit, speaking and teaching diligently the things of the Lord, knew only the baptism of John! Paul was comfortable with the faith of these disciples else would he have re-baptized them in the name of the Lord Jesus Christ that they could receive the infilling of the Holy Spirit? If they were only being saved, then Paul was guilty of baptizing a group of unconverted men!

FINALLY — that receiving the Holy Spirit refers to something more than being born again by the Spirit and led by the Spirit is testified to by no less authority that the Lord Jesus himself.

John 14:15-17

15 If ye love me, keep my commandments.

16 And I will pray the Father, and he shall give you another Comforter, that he may abide with you for ever;

17 Even the Spirit of truth; **whom the world cannot receive, because it seeth him not, neither knoweth him:** *but ye know him; for he dwelleth with you, and shall be in you. (KJV)*

Jesus clearly states that the world ***(the unsaved/unregenerate) cannot receive the Holy Ghost!*** One must know Him before receiving Him. One must have the Spirit with him before he can have the Spirit in him. It is the believer alone who is in a position to receive the Holy Spirit.

John 14:17

Even the Spirit of truth; whom the world cannot receive, because it seeth him not, neither knoweth him: but ye know him; for he dwelleth with you, and shall be in you. (KJV)

Acts 8:15-17

15 Who, when they were come down, prayed for them, that they might receive the Holy Ghost:

16 (For as yet he was fallen upon none of them: only they were baptized in the name of the Lord Jesus.)

17 Then laid they their hands on them, and they received the Holy Ghost.

Acts 19:2

He said unto them, Have ye received the Holy Ghost since ye believed? And they said unto him, We have not so much as heard whether there be any Holy Ghost. (KJV)

Gal 3:14

That the blessing of Abraham might come on the Gentiles through Jesus Christ; that we might receive the promise of the Spirit through faith. (KJV)

In each of these biblical cases it is made clear that it is the believer alone who is in a position to receive the Holy Spirit. It is no accident that the inspired writers of the New Testament chose the figures of **BIRTH of the Spirit** to represent regeneration and **BAPTISM of the Spirit** to describe the fullness of the indwelling Spirit of God in the believer.

Obviously, in the order of nature, a **Birth must precede a Baptism** .....one has to be born before he can be baptized! Here then is the logic of example.

Each instance was characterized by immediacy. Each took place at a given point in the experience of the person involved. Nowhere is there a trace of sanctification by growth, by a long and painful process of self-discipline, never completed until death.

In the final analysis, all theories of sanctification must recognize its instantaneity. If sanctification is at physical death, or at the resurrection, it must occur in an instant! Even if it were by growth, there must be a moment when full growth is attained. The debate centers about the issue as to WHEN that completing instant occurs.

To this I unhesitatingly affirm, the testimony of God's Word is final. The hour of full salvation is not some remote future hour. The day of deliverance from all carnal sin is not some far-off day. Every divine imperative, every command of God is for the ***present moment, never for the future.***

2 Cor 6:2

...: behold, now is the accepted time; behold, now is the day of salvation.) (KJV)

Rom 12:1

I beseech you therefore, brethren, by the mercies of God, that ye present your bodies a living sacrifice, holy, acceptable unto God, which is your reasonable service. (KJV)

Points To Ponder

1. Holiness — a journey or an act ? Is it either or could it be both ? ______________________________

____

____

2. In a nutshell what is a brief definition of the Gnostic Theory ? ______________________________

____

____

____

3. According to I Thess. 4:1 – 4 what parts of man does Paul pray will be sanctified ? ________________,
________________, and ________________ .

4. How much of each of these parts does God want sanctified ? ______________________________

____

____

5. Who does this scripture tell us will do the sanctifying ?

____

____

6. When a person is saved, in what we term the New Birth, is that person saved instantaneously when he meets God's conditions or are they saved over a period of time?______________________________

____

____

____

____

____

7. According to John 14, 17, and Act 8:15 –17, and Acts 19:2 who are those who are eligible to received the gift of the Holy Spirit ?______________________________

8. Would you agree that a "birth" must precede a "baptism" ? Could a "baptism" take place if there were nothing born to be baptized ?______________________

9. What would be the spiritual lesson gleaned from the evident answer to the preceding question ? __________

10. When God gave the world John 3:16 was it over a progression of time ?

How about the gift of the Holy Ghost ? Does a gift given and received take place simultaneously?